Old-Time
Meatless Recipes

Books by Katharine Morrison McClinton

A HANDBOOK OF POPULAR ANTIQUES

ANTIQUE COLLECTING FOR EVERYONE

COLLECTING AMERICAN GLASS

COMPLETE BOOK OF
SMALL ANTIQUES COLLECTING

COMPLETE BOOK OF
SMALL COUNTRY ANTIQUES

COLLECTING
AMERICAN VICTORIAN ANTIQUES

COLLECTING
19TH CENTURY AMERICAN SILVER

ANTIQUES OF AMERICAN CHILDHOOD

Old-Time Meatless Recipes,

MENUS,

AND KITCHEN ANTIQUES

Originally entitled *Loaves and Fishes*

by

KATHARINE MORRISON McCLINTON

With drawings of old kitchens of different countries and pottery and porcelain dishes in the shapes of food.
Preface includes notes on old time kitchens and ceramics.

GRAMERCY PUBLISHING COMPANY · NEW YORK

To

H. L. McC.

who provides the ingredients

Copyright © MCMLV, by
Katharine Morrison McClinton
ALL RIGHTS RESERVED
This edition published by Gramercy Publishing Company,
a division of Crown Publishers, Inc.,
by arrangement with the author
e f g h

Printed in the United States of America

Notes

on the ILLUSTRATIONS of OLD-TIME KITCHENS and POTTERY and PORCELAIN in the SHAPES of FOOD.

There was a time in the early days of America when the daily life of the household centered in the kitchen. Here, to the tune of the simmering kettle, the woman of the house spun the material for garments, at the same time watching the baby cradled near by. Here the butter was churned and moulded in hand carved butter molds. Here the guests were received and on the wooden settle beside the low fireplace the young girl received her beau. There was a charm about the simple life lived in these old-time kitchens. Each article was made for its usefulness and resulted in a certain naive beauty.

Life in the early Dutch household also centered in the kitchen, but the spirit of industry and cleanliness often overruled that of comfort and quiet peace. When we enter a Dutch kitchen we notice first the colored tiles shining like glass, the brass and pewter gleaming like gold and silver. The general effect is cheerfulness, color and neatness. Everything is in its place, and the Dutch housewife is often known to have given her family a warmed-over meal rather than soil her tiled hearth. The Dutch kitchen is fitted with all the pots and pans dear to the heart of the housewife—cauldrons, churns, kettles, bellows, and spits are all there. And the cupboards contain everything necessary for cooking and cleaning.

I have another kitchen in mind, a sweet "homely" place in Chester. There was a stone flagged floor, and a beamed ceiling of age-blackened oak. Many kinds of burnished copper vessels adorned the walls. Here, after a ramble across twilight fields to hear the nightingales sing in the copses, we gathered about an oak table in front of the stone fireplace and refreshed ourselves with a typical English ten-o'clock supper of bread and butter, brawn, cheese, and salad. The spirit of this kitchen was dignified, yet simple.

5

A Swedish kitchen with its corner fireplace and wall bed opposite where one might lie and watch the dying coals, and with its comfortable log armchair, the forerunner of our winged fireside chairs, surely bespeaks true comfort. And if one chances to see the lazy farmer dozing with a cat at his feet and the flies slowly circling in the center of the room, the picture of comfort seems complete. In some houses the walls have weathered a luscious golden brown of the natural wood, for these walls are given no other finish than a varnish of pine oils. On a feast day old "Bonaden" paintings on canvas are hung on the walls, and perhaps the finest specimens of the father's wood carving and the mother's weaving are brought out to exhibit to visiting neighbors and relatives.

The enormous hooded fireplace of the gracious Spanish kitchen is in winter the gathering place for the whole family. Built-in cushioned seats beneath the fireplace hood allow ample seating room. And one does not wonder that the men love to gather there to entertain their wives with their interpretation of the day's events, so coupled with superstition that it becomes a story in the telling. Meanwhile the wife is preparing well-seasoned food, or perhaps salting pork on the *tocinera,* a table gaining its name with the process. Although the walls of the Spanish kitchen are whitewashed with lime, they are relieved by the use of colorful tile in the chimney end of the room and by many patterned and brilliant pieces of Talavera pottery. Sometimes the kitchen is literally wainscotted with pots and pans or kitchen utensils, hanging upon an *espetera* of spiral iron.

Sitting in a tassel-backed chair before a huge Normandy fireplace, with one's back to the warm coals, is a simple comfort fit for kings. *La maison* is an important room, for it serves all purposes of the peasant family. Every home in Normandy has three favorite pieces—the table, the buffet, and the grandfather's clock; but to me the hooded fireplace with its checked gingham ruffle, which is repeated at the small-paned windows, suggests the real spirit and atmosphere of the old-time Normandy kitchen. Simple, rustic, naively artistic, yet unlike other peasant kitchens, there is a certain chic in the characteristic old-time maison of Normandy.

In sunny Italy, where summer finds the family doorstep crowded, the kitchen again forms the scene of the life of the household within, and in winter the fireplace, with its built-in seats, is the center of that scene. One always finds a colorful picture—peasant costumes and green and red strings of drying peppers and herbs. Cat, dog, chicken, and even goat join the Italian fireside group. A certain strength and robustness seem to exude in the atmosphere of such a scene. Of all peasant kitchens, those of Italy are the most picturesque.

Many of the recipes in this book are from old-time kitchens such as these described. They were taken from English and American cookbooks of the eighteenth and nineteenth centuries and from old manuscripts. Old cook books often give unique ideas, but the recipes must be tested and adapted to present day ingredients. I have sometimes changed ingredients and have often added herbs and wine. Cheese-Wine Toast on page 45 and Marmalade Apple Pie, page 104, were taken from "The Cooks Own Book," published by Monroe & Francis in Boston in 1838. Daniel Webster Chowder, page 38, came from an original manuscript in The New-York Historical Society as did Roman Punch, which was served at Castle Garden, New York, in 1848. The recipe was taken from the *Castle Garden Record Book,* which is in the collection of The New-York Historical Society. Potage Royale, page 85, was from an old Jewish cookbook which was privately printed in Seattle, Washington and Chili Beans, page 50, was taken from a hand-written New Mexican cookbook.

Some of the most intriguing articles for the collector of antiques are those that were used in the old-time kitchen. These include kitchen utensils and pots, kettles and molds for preparing and serving foods. They were made in many different materials, including tin, iron, copper, brass and various kinds of ceramics from primitive redware and stoneware pottery to fine porcelain.

Some of the most interesting tinware articles are those used on the hearth. These include tin ovens, bakers and coffee-bean roasters. There were also tin coffee pots, pie pans, muffin pans, cake and pudding molds, measures, dippers, strainers, and cottage cheese molds in round, square, diamond and heart shapes. Pie crimpers for edging a pie were made of wood with tin wheels.

Tin cookie molds are a category to themselves. Their fascinating shapes range from stars, crescents, hearts, flowers and animals to human figures, including a Revolutionary soldier, William Penn and Uncle Sam. Kitchen articles of wood include butter churns, mortars, bowls, scoops, plates, spoons, mugs and spice boxes. The woods used included apple, ash, birch, beech, basswood, cherry, hickory, maple, oak, pine, poplar and walnut. The carved spoon rack was a popular article. These racks are decorated with scratch carving and often marked with dates and names. Another woodenware kitchen article popular with collectors today is the butter mold. These were hand-cut in designs including geometric stars, pineapple and other fruits, a sheaf of wheat, eagles, doves, sheep and cows. Pennsylvania Dutch designs included hearts, tulips, hex signs and three feathers. There were also woodenware rolling pins and carved springerle and marzipan molds.

Iron cooking utensils included forks, ladles, skewers, trammels and pots, kettles and spiders of various sizes. There were also iron trivets and gridirons for use on the hearth.

Skimmers and ladles were also made of copper and brass, and there were copper measures, tea kettles and cake pans.

Pottery made for use in the kitchen included dishes of slipware with inscriptions such as the pie plates marked with the owner's name or those marked "Apple Pie," "Shoo Fly" or "Mince Pie." Stoneware crocks, jugs, jars and pitchers, churns, cake molds and bean pots were decorated with incised and painted designs, and some have dates and are stamped with the maker's name. Cake and pudding molds were made in cream, yellow, brown and red glazed earthenware. In shape they are round, oval, oblong and melon. The mold designs include flowers, vegetables such as corn, grapes, pineapple, a frog, and geometric patterns. Brown Rockingham cooking were made in Ohio; Bennington and other potteries included pudding and jelly molds, baking dishes and pie plates. More sophisticated molds were made by European potters, including Wedgwood.

The illustrations in this book are from sketches made in museums, shops, and private collections in this country and abroad. They are for the most part of the eighteenth century pottery and porcelain, although a few sketches illustrate glass objects. Dishes made in the shapes of the food that was served in them date as early as the fifteenth century in Europe and were used even earlier in China, but the period when they were especially popular was the eighteenth century. Plates were molded in leaf forms, and tureens of all sizes were made in the shapes of vegetables such as cabbage, asparagus, artichoke, or lettuce. Or they might be in fruit forms such as melon, pineapple, pear, apple, or lemons. Tureens in which meat was served took the form of turkeys, chickens, geese, hams, and wild boars heads. There were lifelike pigeon tureens for pigeon stew, and rabbit tureens for the favorite civet of hare. There were also tureens and serving platters in the forms of various kinds of fish, including eel.

In the seventeenth century enamelled pottery table services were made in Germany in the forms of animals and vegetables, and such forms as hams, boars heads, and melons were often found. In Brussels, Belgium, in the eighteenth century faience tureens in the forms of asparagus, cabbages, melons, artichokes, pigeons, cocks, turkeys, and eels were in popular usage. Similar articles were made at Rouen, Marseilles, and Strasbourg in France, and in Delft and other cities in Holland. Delft faience is well known, and articles such as tureens in the shape of purple grapes, apples, and lemons were popular. Ducks of various sizes sit in faience nests, and rabbit tureens were also made in several sizes.

Similar pottery shapes were also made in Denmark, Sweden, Portugal, Spain, and Italy. In Spain, plates holding red and green faience peppers were characteristic, and tureens in the forms of fish were especially popular in the Roman Catholic, Latin-European lands of Spain, Portugal, and Italy.

The popular melon tureen was made in all these potteries. Sometimes it was naturalistic in color, or it might be a brilliant turquoise glaze, as the pair of Brussels faience melon tureens which I saw recently. Melon tureens were also made in cream-colored Queensware by Wedgwood, and of Leeds, Castleford, and Liverpool cream wares. Wedgwood also made teapots and coffee pots in the forms of pineapples and cauliflower in cream color and in naturalistic colors.

One of the most interesting serving dishes was the Game Pie dish used for baking the game pies, and which was made to imitate the crust of the game pie. In 1815, when there was a shortage of flour because of the Napoleonic Wars, these dishes supplied the need and took over the job of the baker for a few years. In addition to the imitation crust they were decorated with hare and bird designs in relief, and usually the cover of the dish had a molded rabbit or bird's head. These were used for baking the popular English game pies.

The most elaborate game and vegetable tureens were made of porcelain, especially Meissen and Chelsea porcelain. The Meissen fruits are rich in color and decoration. There were small covered apples, pears, citrons, and lemons, and larger melon tureens, and duck, swan, and hen-and-chick covered tureens. Finials and handles of these tureens were of delicate trailing vines, and a realistic snail, bird, or caterpillar might be set on a cover of an artichoke or melon tureen.

Chelsea porcelain fruit and vegetable forms were similar to those made of Meissen porcelain. There were melons, lettuce, asparagus, figs, grapes, lemons, pears, and pomegranates in tureen form for use at the table. Chelsea apples had a naturalistic caterpillar finial, and artichokes might have a tiny bird atop their covers. There were also tureens in the shape of pineapples, red cabbages, lettuce, cauliflower and asparagus. A tiny porcelain green pea is also characteristic of Chelsea porcelain. The game tureens of Chelsea porcelain are the most elaborate. There were rabbits, pigeons, ducks, drakes, swans, partridges, cocks, hens, and boars head tureens in various sizes. These are naturalistic in shape, but usually decorated with flower and leaf designs. Similar porcelain tureens were also made of Bow, Derby, and Longton Hall porcelain in the mid-eighteenth century.

In the nineteenth century both fruit and vegetable forms were made in majolica. Many of these were copies of the earlier Wedgwood pineapple and cabbage forms, such as teapots and coffee pots. These were made in England, on the Continent, and in America. One individual and truly American form was the majolica ear-of-corn pitcher which originated in Ohio.

Melon and fish forms were made in America in milk glass. These were usually in blue or opaque white. Covered dishes with setting hens, birds, swans, rabbits, cats or dogs were also made in nineteenth-century milk glass. There were various covered dishes in fish shapes and uncovered fish-shaped pickle and relish dishes. Similar milk-glass dishes were also made in England, France, and other countries, and while many were made for serving foods, others were used as pin or jewelry boxes. The illustrations in this book show only the pieces used to serve food.

—K. M. McC.

Contents

Part One

Cooking with Herbs

HERBS CHANGE the flavor and add variety to the taste of ordinary foods. Herbs may be used in salads, soups, stews, and in all kinds of meat, fish, and vegetable dishes. Herbs add no calories to the diet, but some herbs contain valuable vitamins, and the savor that herbs give to many otherwise tasteless foods certainly sharpens the appetite and relieves the flatness of everyday cooking. Which herb is most used depends upon your own individual preference. Tradition combines such herbs as dill, basil, and tarragon with salads. Sage, marjoram, thyme, and parsley are known as meat flavorings; and basil, fennel, and dill adapt themselves to fish. However, the French chef cannot cook without his chervil, the Italian cook uses oregano for his pizza and spaghetti, and the German cook cannot get along without anise and caraway. Any original or inventive cook will experiment with his or her own choice of herbs.

There is indeed an art in using and blending herbs. The herb should never overpower the real taste of the food, and generally speaking, herbs should be used with a light hand. By tasting and testing you will soon produce your own favorite blends. Try dropping sprigs of fresh green herbs over meats and fish while broiling or barbecuing. They will burn, but will impart a delicate flavor. Try minced oregano, lovage, and savory, or a combination of minced rosemary, chives, and parsley, and mix these with hamburgers or chopped steak before broiling. Or make slits in lamb and put in garlic, rosemary, and sage leaves. Cook ham with rosemary and dry red wine. Sprigs of herbs such as tarragon, basil, savory, and parsley, may be added to green salad. Also minced herbs may be added to cream cheeses and other cheeses to make your own individual blend.

Herbs may also be used in combinations known as "Fines Herbes," a term given to a combination of tarragon, chives, chervil, and shallots, or basil, savory, parsley, and chives. In *The Cooks Own Book,* published in Boston in 1838, we find "Herbs, A Bunch of Sweet, is made up of parsley, sweet marjoram, winter savory, orange and lemon thyme, the greatest proportion of parsley." A "Bouquet Garni" is a term given to such varied combinations as parsley, thyme, onion, and a bay leaf, or marjoram, savory, fennel, basil, leeks or a vegetable. A "Bouquet" of basil, thyme, savory, and marjoram is excellent to flavor a tomato dish. For homemade consomme try a "bouquet" of parsley, celery leaves, thyme, sweet marjoram, sage, savory, and bay leaves. For fish stock make a "bouquet of celery, parsley leaves, ½ teaspoon sage and savory, 2 bay leaves, 3 pepper corns, and 3 cloves. Put this in a bag and when stock is done remove bag of herbs.

Herbs and vegetables are also used as garnishes. A garnish makes a bright color contrast to decorate the plate, please the eye, and pique the appetite. Crisp bouquets of watercress, sprigs of parsley, and such vegetables as celery, cucumbers, olives, cherry tomatoes, pickles, and carrots may be used as garnishes. Lemons, oranges, and cherries are well-known garnishes, also fruits such as pineapple, apricots, prunes, or apples may be sliced, glazed, or spiced, and used as garnishes. Relishes are also used as garnishes and appetite whetters, and their appearance as well as their taste is pleasing. Jellies and pickles may also be used as garnishes. However, a sprig of fresh mint, or a bit of parsley, or a few chopped chives put herbs in first place as garnishes.

The following is a list of the most common herbs and seasonings and their uses:

Anise—Sweet leaves used in fruit salads, vegetables, soups, and stews. Seeds used in cakes, cookies, fruits, and sausages.

Basil—Tastes and smells like cloves. Delicious in salads and all tomato and potato dishes. In soups, meat and game and in spaghetti and noodles with tomato sauce.

Bay Leaf—For fish, game, salads, stews. In eggs, stews, and sauces, and sweet vegetables such as eggplant, green peppers; and cream cheese.

Burnet—For salads, tomatoes, and in sour cream dressings.

Caraway—In breads, cookies. In cheese, cabbage, or potatoes.

Coriander—Seeds are used to flavor sausages, cheese, pickles. Also may be used in soups and salads.

Chervil—Salads, soups, pot roast. Has a licorice flavor.

Chives—Salads; also seasoning for fish, or eggs.

Cummin—An herb spice used to season cheese, eggs, meats, and vegetables.

Curry—In meat and fish curries. In salad dressings.

Dill—For fish and fish sauces, potato and vegetable salad, cole slaw, cucumbers, and cheese spreads. A sweet-bitter flavor.

Fennel—Has a pungent, sweet odor and taste. Used for fish, salads, and soups.

Garlic—Use with or in place of onions for heightened flavor.

Marjoram—Seasoning for meats, poultry, omelets, and cheese dishes. For carrots and mushrooms.

Mint—Seasoning in drinks, with fruit, and with vegetables to serve with lamb.

Nutmeg—For custards, pies, stewed fruits, sauces, and vegetables.

Oregano—For Italian dishes such as spaghetti and pizza. For meat balls, meatloaf, stews, soups, fish, vegetables such as tomatoes and squash.

Paprika—Eggs, fish, stews, poultry, salads, appetisers, and cheese.

Parsley—For seasoning and garnishing. Combines with all other herbs.

Rosemary—For meats with parsley and garlic. In sauces, in biscuits, to flavor string beans, and salads.

Sage—For stuffings for poultry and goose. In soups, onions, and try with cottage cheese.

Savory—A peppery flavor. In stuffings, meatballs, and meat loaf. To season vegetables such as beans, squash, or eggplant.

Shallot—Use instead of onions.

Tarragon—For fish and all seafood; chicken, eggs, mushrooms, spinach, celery, and tomatoes.

Thyme—For oyster stew or clam chowder, for meats and vegetables such as carrots, peas, eggplant and onions. Thyme tastes like it smells. Combines well with parsley and sorrel.

The Herb Garden

We remember the fish which we did eat in Egypt freely; the cucumbers, and the melons, and the leeks, and the onions, and the garlick.—NUMBERS 11:5

IN BIBLICAL DAYS, orchards, herb gardens, and vineyards were the representative gardens. They were pleasure gardens laid out in formal patterns and adorned with fountains and pavillions. They were not only for beauty, but for use as well. Herb gardens were laid out in formal beds; and roses, lilies, violets, iris, and other flowers were grown among the herbs. The plan of these gardens often followed that of an interlaced square or knotted garden of geometrical design, with the broad lines planted with some low growing shrub or herb, such as box or thyme, marjoram, savory, or yew or santolina. The interstices of the design were filled with flowers, and beds were usually planted all of one color. In England, walls, or "wall herbers," were made of rosemary, lavender, jasmine, or musk roses.

Later the growing of herbs gradually became concentrated in the kitchen garden with the salad greens and other vegetables. In Stuart England, "simple salads" consisted of chives, boiled carrots, turnips, lettuces, asparagus, purslane, etc., chopped and served with leaves of red sage, mint, lettuce, violets, marigolds and spinach. The herbs planted in the old English kitchen gardens were cole warts, endive, sow thistle, succory, globe artichokes, sorrel, burnet, marigolds, beets, blites, arrach, spinach, borage, bugloss, leeks, purslane, onions, chives, garlic, parsley, rocket, tarragon, smallage, chervil, costmary, cress, asparagus, saffron, turnips, radishes, parsnips, carrots, skirrits, mustard, poppies, cucumbers, and gourds. Herbs were also grown for nosegays and for sweet smells, and in the olden days, pots of herbs such as rosemary, sage, thyme, marjoram, parsley, winter savory, watercress, and leeks were sold in London streets.

Today your herb garden may be a part of your flower garden, or it may be a small separate plot with only a few selected herbs planned to serve your special cooking needs. Of course, it is best to have the culinary herb garden convenient to the house, and as near the kitchen door as possible. If the herb garden is to be a small plot in the garden there are many plans and designs available. There may be small symmetrical beds with each herb in its own plot. A simple square may be divided into different shaped beds by the use of bricks, or a larger space could be divided with gravel walks. If the herb garden is large enough, the center may be filled with a sun dial or a fountain which would provide water for luxuriant mint and cresses. Herbs may also be planted in the garden beds along with other flowers.

If you have a barbecue terrace, the herbs might be planted in beds around the terrace so that they are close at hand for the outdoor cook. For garden planting the large herbs such as oregano, rosemary, tarragon, winter savory, and sage should be planted at the back of the bed so that they can be allowed to grow tall, and the smaller herbs can be planted at the front and used as borders.

Herbs may also be grown in the kitchen window and the box placed on the outside sill during the warm months and moved to the inside in the winter. It is most satisfactory if small plants are planted in the window box in early Spring or September. You can get perennial plants of rosemary, tarragon, thyme, mint, sage, and chervil. Chives may be added to the box, and in the spring, dill and basil plants. Pick a cool window with some sunlight, and water regularly. On warm days open the window for fresh air. I have had a window box of herbs in my kitchen window (outside in summer, inside in winter) in New York City for the past three years. With all due credit to the commercial dried herbs, there is nothing like a few leaves of fresh sage cut up, together with minced garlic and butter, spread on top of chicken before it is broiled. Then I reach to my window box and snip off a sprig of tarragon or a few leaves of fresh basil and add them to my green salad, or I add a few rosemary leaves to the sauce in which I marinate my steak.

Of course, parsley and chives are used more than any other herb, but these can usually be obtained from the grocer the year round and for this reason hardly deserve space in a small window box.

You will find that chopped mint goes in carrots as well as peas, and a fresh mint sauce may be made to serve on grapefruit. You will want dill and tarragon for salads and fish, and thyme and perhaps a few scented geraniums for use at the tea table. Our grandmothers put the leaves in jelly and custards and on the bottom of cup cake pans.

Fish Sauce Recipes

Almond Butter Sauce
½ cup butter
½ cup blanched almonds sliced
1 teaspoon onion juice
1 teaspoon chopped chives
1 teaspoon lemon juice
Dash each of salt, pepper & nutmeg.

Melt butter in saucepan and add other ingredients stirring constantly.

Anchovy Sauce
2 teaspoons anchovies mashed with fork
¾ cup melted butter
¼ cup sherry

Simmer over fire, add salt and pepper and 1 teaspoon lemon juice.

Bechamel Caper Sauce
2 tablespoons butter   ¼ cup flour
¼ small onion minced   1 pt. milk

Cook onion in butter and add flour then milk.
Add ¼ cup chopped capers, 1½ teaspoon lemon juice, salt, pepper, parsley.

Bercy Sauce
1 cup Bechamel Caper Sauce (see above)
½ cup fish stock
3 tablespoons melted butter
1 teaspoon chopped parsley
salt, pepper

Mix all ingredients together and pour over fish and brown under the broiler.

Bernaise Sauce

To Hollandaise Sauce add:

>1 teaspoon minced fresh tarragon
>1 teaspoon minced fresh thyme
>1 teaspoon fresh chopped parsley

Caper Sauce

>¼ pound butter
>1 tablespoon lemon juice
>¼ cup capers
>1 teaspoon minced parsley
>salt & pepper to taste

Cucumber Sauce

>1 teaspoon lemon juice
>1 teaspoon grated onion
>½ teaspoon salt
>¾ cup olive oil
>cayenne, thyme

Blend together, then add:

>¼ teaspoon dry mustard
>½ cup diced cucumbers

Serve cold.

Curry Sauce

>½ cup chopped onions
>3 tablespoons butter
>1 cup cubed green apples

Cook together. Remove from fire and sprinkle with mixture of:

>2 tablespoons flour
>2 teaspoons curry powder
>½ teaspoon salt
>¼ teaspoon nutmeg & cayenne

Scald 1½ cups milk, 1 slice garlic, 1 bay leaf, 6 slices onion, 1 teaspoon chopped parsley. Strain and add. Boil sauce until it thickens.

Herb Mayonnaise

    1 cup mayonnaise
    1 teaspoon chopped chives
    1 teaspoon chopped tarragon leaves
    2 teaspoons chopped parsley
    1 teaspoon chopped dill

Mix together.

Herb Sauce

    ½ cup butter melted
    ⅓ cup white wine

Add:

    1 teaspoon chopped parsley
    1 teaspoon chopped chives
    1 teaspoon terragon & chervil mixed

Horseradish Sauce

To one cup cream sauce add:

    2 tablespoons fresh grated horseradish
    1 teaspoon minced parsley
    ½ teaspoon paprika

Frozen Horseradish Sauce I

    3 tablespoons butter
    3 tablespoons flour
    1½ cup milk
    1½ cups chicken broth
    2 cups cream
    ¾ cup fresh grated horseradish
    6 tablespoons vinegar

Melt butter, add flour, and pour on milk and chicken broth. Cool, freeze, and while soft add beaten cream, horseradish and seasonings. Freeze to consistency of thick cream and serve.

Frozen Horseradish Sauce II
    1 pt. cream
    6 heaping tablespoons freshly grated horseradish
    ½ teaspoon French mustard
    salt, pepper

Whip cream stiff, add other ingredients and freeze in ice try. Slice and serve on lettuce leaves.

Lemon Sauce
    2 lemons
    2 egg yolks
    1 teaspoon sugar
    1 cup hot fish stock
    1 teaspoon chopped parsley

Mix grated rind of lemons and egg yolks. Add lemon juice and pour on fish stock. Cook until thick, stirring constantly. Add sugar and parsley. Serve.

Maitre D'Hotel Sauce
    ½ cup butter
    1 tablespoon chopped parsley
    ½ teaspoon paprika
    salt, pepper
    juice ½ lemon

Cream all ingredients together and make into balls.

Mustard Sauce
    2 teaspoons Bahamian mustard
    6 tablespoons melted butter

Mix and serve.

Sauce Meunière
    ¼ lb. melted butter, browned
    1 tablespoon lemon juice
    1 teaspoon chopped parsley

Combine and serve.

Fish Sauce Recipes

Sauce Normandy

  2 tablespoons melted butter
  1 teaspoon flour
  1 cup fish & mushroom liquor
  2 egg yolks
  ½ cup cream

Cook butter and flour in saucepan until golden. Add liquor and cook 10 minutes. Mix egg yolks and cream and combine with sauce. Strain and serve with fish or oysters.

Shallot Sauce

  2 tablespoons chopped shallots boiled and drained
  6 tablespoons butter
  1 teaspoon lemon juice

Strain through sieve.

Tomato Sauce

Cook together until onion browns:
  3 tablespoons olive oil
  1 clove garlic, chopped
  1 large Bermuda Onion, chopped
  ½ green pepper
  1 carrot

Add:

  1 qt. chopped tomatoes
  1 bay leaf
  4 sprigs parsley
  1 sprig thyme
  6 pepper corns, salt

Cook slowly 30 minutes until thickens, strain, and serve.

French Dressing
Variations

Caraway and Celery Salad Dressing
    1 cup olive oil
    ½ cup lemon juice
    ½ teaspoon salt
    ⅛ teaspoon pepper
    ¼ teaspoon caraway seeds
    ¼ teaspoon celery salt
    ½ clove garlic

Mix until thoroughly blended.

Curry French Dressing
    1 cup olive oil
    ½ cup vinegar or lemon juice
    ½ teaspoon salt
    ½ clove garlic
    1 tablespoon chopped shallots
    1 teaspoon curry
    ¼ teaspoon ground pepper

Mix until thoroughly blended.

French Dressing I
    ¾ cup olive oil
    ¼ cup vinegar
    ¼ teaspoon salt
    ⅛ teaspoon ground pepper
    1 clove garlic

Beat mixture with a fork until it thickens and let stand several hours before using.

French Dressing II

    9 tablespoons olive oil
    3 tablespoons red wine vinegar
    1 small onion chopped
    1 clove garlic
    ½ teaspoon mustard
    ½ teaspoon Worcestershire sauce
    1 teaspoon salad herbs
    1 teaspoon salt
    freshly ground black pepper

Mash onion and garlic, add mustard, salt, Worcestershire sauce, and vinegar. Beat in oil and add herbs and black pepper.

French Dressing with Dill

    1 cup olive oil
    ½ cup dry vermouth
    ½ teaspoon salt
    ⅛ teaspoon pepper
    1 shallot
    ½ clove garlic
    2 teaspoon chopped dill leaves

Mix until thoroughly blended.

French Dressing with Oregano

    1 cup wine vinegar
    2 cups olive oil
    ½ teaspoon dry mustard
    1½ teaspoon oregano
    ¼ teaspoon salt
    pepper
    ½ teaspoon Worcestershire sauce
    ½ teaspoon chopped garlic

Mix until thoroughly blended.

Lemon French Dressing

⅔ cup olive oil
⅓ cup lemon juice
¼ teaspoon sugar
1 teaspoon salt
⅛ teaspoon black pepper
1 clove garlic
¼ teaspoon dry mustard.

Mix until thoroughly blended.

Lemon-Orange French Dressing

¼ cup lemon juice
¼ cup orange juice
½ cup olive oil
2 tablespoons sugar
½ teaspoon salt
1 teaspoon paprika
¼ teaspoon freshly ground pepper

Mix until thoroughly blended.

Red Wine Salad Dressing

1 cup salad oil
⅓ cup red wine vinegar
2 tablespoons red wine
¼ teaspoon mustard
½ teaspoon salt
¼ teaspoon paprika
½ clove garlic
pepper

Mix until thoroughly blended.

Roquefort Dressing

¼ lb. Roquefort cheese
¼ teaspoon paprika
½ teaspoon Worcestershire sauce
1 tablespoon tarragon vinegar, salt
½ cup olive oil
½ teaspoon dry mustard
1 tablespoon lemon juice

Mash cheese thoroughly with a fork. Add olive oil and dry ingredients and stir until smooth.

31

Salad Dressing

    1 cup olive oil
    ½ cup wine vinegar
    ¼ teaspoon pepper
    ¼ teaspoon paprika
    ½ teaspoon sugar
    1 egg yolk
    4 fillets of anchovies

Mix dry ingredients with yolk of egg, add vinegar then oil.

Sherry Salad Dressing

    1 cup olive oil
    ¼ cup white wine vinegar
    ¼ cup dry sherry
    ½ teaspoon salt
    ⅛ teaspoon pepper
    2 teaspoons chopped chervil
    ground pepper

Mix until thoroughly blended.

Tarragon Salad Dressing

    1 cup olive oil
    ½ cup tarragon vinegar
    ½ teaspoon salt
    ⅛ teaspoon pepper
    1 teaspoon chopped tarragon leaves
    1 chopped shallot

Mix until thoroughly blended.

West Indies French Dressing

    1 cup olive oil
    ½ cup vinegar
    ¼ teaspoon salt
    ⅛ teaspoon pepper
    1 clove garlic

    ½ teaspoon paprika
    2 teaspoons each:
    chopped shallots
    green pepper
    parsley

Mix until thoroughly blended.

Part Two

Luncheon

GRAND CENTRAL OYSTER STEW*

CRACKERS   HORSERADISH

COFFEE

Grand Central Oyster Stew

    1 tablespoon butter
    6 or 7 fresh oysters
    ½ teaspoon paprika
    1 teaspoon Worcestershire sauce
    ½ cup clam juice
    ¾ cup milk
    celery salt, pepper

Put butter, paprika, Worcestershire sauce, and clam juice in pan. Stir until butter melts and ingredients are well mixed, then add oysters and cook 1 or 2 minutes. Add milk, celery salt, and pepper, and cook until oyster edges curl (only 1 or 2 minutes more).

Serve immediately in bowl with 1 tablespoon butter and paprika on top. This makes a large bowl for one person. Cream may be substituted for milk.

Oyster Plate—
19th Century American

Luncheon

PEPPERS STUFFED WITH FISH*

BANANA SPONGE PUDDING*

COFFEE

Peppers Stuffed with Fish

Scoop out seeds of peppers and parboil 15 minutes. Fill with mixture of leftover fish broken in small pieces, salt, pepper, grated cheese, and cream sauce. Put bread crumbs on top of each pepper and dot with butter. Bake in oven until brown and peppers are done (about 20 minutes). Serve with tomato sauce.

Banana Sponge Pudding

```
1 cup mashed bananas
½ tablespoon gelatine
4 tablespoons cold water
¼ cup boiling water
½ cup confectioners' sugar
3 tablespoons lemon juice
1 egg white
```

Soak gelatine in cold water and then add boiling water to dissolve. Add sugar to banana pulp, then add lemon juice and gelatine. Beat egg white until stiff and add to mixture. Chill in mold and serve with chopped nuts on top.

Luncheon

```
TUNA  FISH  SALAD*

FRENCH BREAD

GARLIC BUTTER

TEA
```

Tuna Fish Salad

    1 can tuna
    1 cucumber, diced
    1 cup of chopped parsley
    1 tablespoon lemon juice
    ½ cup mayonnaise
    salt, pepper
    ½ teaspoon mustard
    lettuce

Flake tuna and combine with ingredients and serve on lettuce leaves.

A New England Kitchen

37

Luncheon

CHOWDER DANIEL WEBSTER*

SHIP BISCUITS

COFFEE

Chowder Daniel Webster

    6 lbs. blue or white fish cut in slices
  25 oysters
    4 tablespoons sautéed onions
    1 qt. boiled mashed potatoes
 1½ lbs. ship biscuits broken
   ½ bottle mushroom catsup
    1 teaspoon thyme
   ½ grated nutmeg (1 teaspoon)
a few cloves, mace, allspice and
      slices of lemon, black pepper
    1 bottle port or claret

Put all ingredients in a pot. Add enough water to cover and cook slowly 1 hour.

Note: This recipe is reprinted from an original manuscript, through the courtesy of the New York Historical Society.

*Fish Tureen—
18th Century Italian*

Luncheon

Peppers Stuffed with Eggs

    6 green peppers
    6 eggs
    1 onion (chopped)
    ¼ cup butter
    1 tablespoon chopped parsley
    ¼ teaspoon salt
    ⅛ teaspoon pepper
    1 teaspoon Worcestershire sauce
    bread crumbs

Seed and parboil peppers. Chop onion and sauté in butter, add parsley and seasoning. Put a spoonful of onion and butter mixture in each pepper. Break one egg on top of mixture in each pepper. Cover with bread crumbs and put remainder of melted butter mixture on top. Bake about 15 minutes. Serve hot with Hollandaise sauce.

Gingerbread with Honey Butter

    To gingerbread mix add:
    3 tablespoons chopped blanched almonds
    2 tablespoons chopped citron
    ½ teaspoon grated orange rind

Bake according to directions on package. Serve hot with honey butter.

Luncheon

MUSHROOM AND CHEESE
CASSEROLE*
GREEN SALAD
STEWED RHUBARB AND
STRAWBERRIES*
COFFEE

Mushrooms and Cheese Casserole

2 lbs. mushrooms
¼ lb. parmesan cheese
¼ lb. Gruyere cheese
4 tablespoons butter

Bechamel Sauce

4 tablespoons butter   salt and pepper
1 onion chopped   1 sprig thyme
4 tablespoons flour   1 bay leaf
2 cups light cream or milk   2 sprigs parsley

Slice mushroom heads and stalks in half. Put in earthenware casserole with butter and sauté until tender. Make Bechamel sauce, using half of each kind of cheese to make sauce. Melt butter and onion, then add flour, milk, cheese, and seasoning. Put layer of mushrooms in casserole, then layer of grated cheese, then layer of Bechamel sauce, and repeat layers until ingredients are used, ending with layer of grated cheese. Brown in oven 5 to 10 minutes.

Stewed Rhubarb and Strawberries

2 lbs. rhubarb   1 box strawberries
½ cup sugar

Wash and cut up rhubarb and cover with water, add sugar. When half done add whole picked strawberries. Cook until strawberries are just done but still whole. Cool and serve.

Luncheon

```
CREAMED VEGETABLE
CASSEROLE*
MIXED GREEN SALAD
WITH SARDINES
ORANGE DATE CUP*
COFFEE
```

Creamed Vegetable Casserole

Use mixture of leftover peas, carrots, lima beans, string beans, beets, or asparagus. Season and mix together with a thick cream sauce. Put in baking casserole and cover top with buttered toast crumbs and a layer of grated "store" cheese. Bake in 350 F. oven for one-half hour.

Orange Date Cup

   6 oranges
   ½ cup shredded blanched almonds
   ¾ cup sliced dates
   ⅔ cup orange juice
   1 tablespoon Grand Marnier

Peel and slice oranges. Add almonds and dates. Pour on orange juice and Grand Marnier and chill thoroughly.

Melon Tureen—
Chelsea Porcelain

Luncheon

CHEESE CREAMED ASPARAGUS*

STEWED FRUIT

TEA

Cheese Creamed Asparagus

1 can asparagus
1 cup cheese cream sauce
3 tablespoons grated parmesan cheese
1 tablespoon chopped parsley
toasted bread

Heat asparagus. Make a cheese sauce and arrange asparagus on toast, pour cheese sauce over, and sprinkle with parmesan cheese and parsley and dot with butter.

*Asparagus Tureen—
Chelsea Porcelain*

Luncheon

Scalloped Oysters

    1 pt. small oysters and liquor
    ½ cup butter
    2 cups cracker crumbs
    salt, pepper
    2 tablespoons parsley
    1 can cream of tomato soup

Combine melted butter, cracker crumbs, and seasoning. Butter a baking dish and put in layer of cracker-crumb mixture, then layer of oysters, then layer of tomato soup combined with oyster liquor, ending with layer of cracker crumbs. Bake in 350 F. oven for about 30 minutes.

Baked Rhubarb

    4 cups rhubarb
    1½ cups sugar
    2 sticks cinnamon
    6 cloves
    1 orange

Put layer of diced, unpealed rhubarb in buttered baking dish. Cover with half of sugar, then unpeeled orange slices and 1 stick of cinnamon and several cloves. Repeat layers until the ingredients are used up. Bake in 350 F. over until tender.

Luncheon

Salmon Ring with Peas

    4 tablespoons butter
    1 tablespoon chopped onion
    1 tablespoon flour
    1 cup light cream
    salt, pepper, rosemary
    1 cup salmon
    4 eggs, separated

Melt butter in saucepan. Add onions and sauté until light brown, then add flour, stirring well. Add cream and cook until thick, then season, remove from fire, and add beaten egg yolks and salmon, and fold in stiffly-beaten egg whites. Pour into buttered ring mold and bake about 40 minutes in 350 F. oven. Turn on plate and fill center with buttered peas sprinkled with finely chopped parsley.

Mocha Rice Pudding

    1 cup cooked rice   ¼ teaspoon salt
    3 eggs, separated   1 cup milk
    ½ cup sugar   1 cup coffee
    ½ teaspoon vanilla

Beat egg yolks and add sugar, salt and vanilla. Combine with scaled milk and coffee and cook, stirring constantly until it thickens. Add rice and turn into buttered baking dish. Beat egg whites until stiff and add ¼ teaspoon vanilla and 3 tablespoons sugar. Put egg whites on top of pudding and brown in moderate oven (350 F.) for 20 minutes.

Luncheon

CHEESE-WINE TOAST*

GREEN SALAD

TEA

Cheese-Wine Toast

    6 slices bread, toasted
    1 cup red wine
    1 cup grated cheddar cheese
    1 tablespoon butter
    3 tablespoons white wine
    1 teaspoon mustard

Soak toast in red wine. In double boiler put butter, cheese, white wine, and mustard. Heat and stir 2 or 3 minutes until well mixed. When mixed, spread on toast and put under broiler to brown.

An English Kitchen

Luncheon

CHEESE SOUFFLÉ*

GREEN SALAD

STEWED FRUIT

TEA

Cheese Soufflé

3 eggs separated
2 cups milk
2 cups grated cheese
4 tablespoons ·butter
4 tablespoons flour
salt, paprika
⅛ teaspoon mustard

Melt butter in saucepan and add flour, then milk and seasonings. When thick, add cheese, and stir until melted. Beat egg yolks and pour cheese sauce mixture over eggs, then fold in egg whites. Pour into buttered casserole and set in pan of water and bake in 350 F. over for 45 minutes. Serve immediately.

Pineapple Tureen—
Chelsea Porcelain

46

Luncheon

Lenten Quiche

Line a pie shell with unbaked pie crust. Spread anchovy oil on pie crust and cover bottom with a layer of anchovy fillets. Cover with slices of Gruyère cheese and pour in mixture of:

4 eggs, beaten	1 cup milk
1 tablespoon flour	1 cup light cream
salt, pepper, cayenne	1½ tablespoons melted butter

Sprinkle top with nutmeg. Cook in 375 F. oven for about 40 minutes. If top is not brown put under broiler to brown.

Apple Ring Pudding

    6 apples
    ¾ cup honey butter
    ½ cup sugar
    1 tablespoon cinnamon
    1 tablespoon grated nutmeg
    ½ cup hot water
    bread crumbs

Peel apples, remove cores, and cut in rings ½ inch thick. Spread each ring with honey butter. Put layer of spread apples in buttered casserole. Mix bread crumbs with sugar, cinnamon, grated nutmeg. Alternate layers of apples with layer of bread crumb mixture. Add ½ cup hot water. Bake in 350 F. oven until apples are tender. Serve with additional honey butter.

Luncheon

OMELET*—SPANISH SAUCE*

BLACKBERRY COBBLER*

COFFEE

Plain Omelet

  4 eggs
  2 tablespoons water or milk
  1 tablespoon butter
  ¾ teaspoon salt
  ⅛ teaspoon pepper

Beat eggs, add liquid and seasoning. Melt butter in pan and add egg mixture. Cook over low heat. When film of egg has formed, lift edge and tilt pan so uncooked egg runs under cooked egg. Repeat until all of mixture is cooked and brown on bottom. Remove with spatula, fold over and serve on platter with Spanish Sauce.

Spanish Sauce

  2 tablespoons butter
  3 onions, sliced
  1 tablespoon chopped green pepper
  ½ lb. mushrooms or 1 small can
  1 cup tomatoes or 4 tablespoons tomato paste
  1 tablespoon chopped parsley
  1 tablespoon Worcestershire sauce
  salt, pepper

Melt butter, add onions, pepper, and mushrooms, and sauté 3 minutes. Then add tomatoes or tomato paste, parsley, and seasoning, and cook a few minutes longer. Serve hot over omelet.

Blackberry Cobbler

  1 box blackberries
  1 tablespoon lemon juice
  1 tablespoon butter
½ cup sugar
  1 teaspoon nutmeg
  flaky pie crust

Make pie crust and line deep baking dish. Fill with berries. Sprinkle with lemon juice, sugar, and nutmeg, and dot with butter. Cover with top crust and bake 35 minutes at 350 F. Serve with cream or hard sauce.

A Spanish Kitchen

Luncheon

CHILI BEANS*

GREEN SALAD

TEA

Chili Beans

2 cans baked beans
2 small onions, minced
1 small green pepper, sliced
1 small can tomatoes
½ teaspoon chili powder
pinch oregano
pinch cummin seed

Sauté onions and pepper in fat. When yellow, add tomatoes, salt, whole ground pepper, chili, oregano, and cummin seed. Let simmer in iron skillet for 1 hour. Add beans and cook in oven in covered pot for 1½ hours for good flavor.

Cabbage Dish—
Winterthur Majolica

Luncheon

Codfish Balls

1 cup shredded codfish
2 cups mashed potatoes
2 tablespoons milk
2 tablespoons butter
1 egg
1 teaspoon minced onion
paprika

Soak fish in water several hours. Drain and flake. Add potatoes, beaten egg, and milk. Sauté onion in butter and add that and seasoning to fish mixture. Shape into cakes and place in refrigerator several hours before rolling in flour and frying. Serve with tomato sauce.

German Cole Slaw

1 small head of cabbage
1 teaspoon salt
1 cup vinegar
½ cup sugar
½ teaspoon pepper
1 onion
3 tablespoons olive oil
¼ cup thinly sliced green pepper

Cut cabbage very fine. Put in salt, mix thoroughly, and let stand several hours. Press down and squeeze to get out brine. Mix vinegar, sugar, oil, etc., and pour on cabbage and mix well. Add green peppers.

Luncheon

CHEESE SOUFFLÉ*

GREEN SALAD

NEW ORLEANS FRUIT
COMPOTE*

COFFEE

Cheese Soufflé
    2 tablespoons butter
    3 tablespoons flour
    6 tablespoons grated cheese
    ½ cup hot milk
    3 eggs separated

Mix butter and flour, add hot milk, and cook until thick. Take off stove and put in cheese and yolks of eggs, then whites beaten stiff. Pour into baking dish and bake in moderate oven (350 F.) about 30 minutes.

New Orleans Fruit Compote
    1 can apricots
    1 can freestone peaches or pineapple
    1 can black cherries (or you can use fresh fruits)
    ½ cup orange juice
    juice of ½ lemon
    2 tablespoons grated orange and lemon rind

Drain fruits and place in casserole and cook in slow oven 1 hour. Mix sugar, orange and lemon juice and pour over fruit. Sprinkle grated rind on top. Serve hot or cold with whipped cream.

Luncheon

EGGS CREOLE*

GREEN SALAD

FRUIT JELLO

TEA OR COFFEE

Eggs Creole

  6 hard boiled eggs
  ½ can tomatoes
  1 green pepper
  2 small onions
  ½ cup bread crumbs
  3 tablespoons butter
  salt, pepper, clove
  1 cup soup stock

Chop onions and green pepper fine and sauté in butter, adding bread crumbs, tomatoes, seasonings, and soup stock. Slice eggs and add to mixture and heat thoroughly.

*Artichoke Dish—
Chelsea Porcelain*

Luncheon

NEAPOLITAN PIZZA*

GREEN SALAD

COFFEE

Neapolitan Pizza
    8 oz. Mozzarella cheese
    4 tomatoes
    salt, pepper
    ½ teaspoon oregano
    ½ cup grated Parmesan cheese
    1 onion grated

Make a biscuit dough using 1½ cups flour, and thinly line a 10" or 12" pie plate. Brush crust with olive oil. Spread thickly with slices of Mozzarella. Cut tomatoes in small pieces and put in layer of tomatoes. Add seasoning and grated onion, and sprinkle with Parmesan cheese. A layer of anchovy may be added if desired. Bake in hot oven (375 F.) for 20 minutes.

*Fruit Bowl—
Italian Majolica*

Luncheon

FLUFFY CHIVE OMELET*

APRICOT JELLY*

COFFEE

Fluffy Chive Omelet

    6 eggs separated
    6 tablespoons milk
 1½ tablespoons butter
    ¾ teaspoon salt
    ⅛ teaspoon pepper
    ¼ cup chopped chives
    1 tablespoon grated onion

Beat egg yolks, add milk, salt, and pepper. Beat egg whites until stiff and foamy, fold in chives and onion. Then fold egg whites and egg yolks together. Melt butter in pan and pour in omelet. Cook over low heat until under side is brown and omelet is puffy. Then place pan in 350 F. oven for 5 minutes. Fold and serve. Serves 4 to 6.

Apricot Jelly

    1 lb. dried apricots
    1 cup sugar
    2 tablespoons gelatine
    ½ cup cold water
    ½ cup chopped blanched almonds

Wash and soak apricots in cold water several hours. Add sugar and boil 1 hour. Strain water and apricots through sieve. Add gelatine which has been softened in cold water. Add chopped almonds. Mold and set in ice box. Serve with whipped cream.

Luncheon

CLAM CHOWDER*

TOASTED CRACKERS

CRANBERRY PIE*

COFFEE

Clam Chowder

1 qt. clams
4 cups diced potatoes
1 sliced onion
1 sliced leek
2 cups clam juice
2 cups milk
2 tablespoons bacon fat
1 cup water
2 tablespoons chopped celery

2 tablespoons chopped parsley
1 tablespoon salt
⅛ teaspoon pepper
½ teaspoon thyme
1 teaspoon paprika
1 tablespoon Worcestershire sauce
1 tablespoon flour

Separate clams from liquor. Sauté onion, celery, and leeks in bacon fat or butter, add flour, potatoes, chopped clams, seasonings, and water. Cook 20 minutes. Add milk and lastly clam liquor, and simmer 30 minutes more.

Cranberry Pie

1½ tablespoons cornstarch
¼ teaspoon salt
¼ teaspoon nutmeg
1½ cups sugar

1½ cups cranberries
1 cup water
1½ tablespoons butter

Mix cornstarch, salt, and nutmeg with sugar. Chop cranberries and add them and water. Pour mixture into 10″ pie plate and dot with butter. Make a criss-cross top crust. Bake in 450 F. oven for 10 minutes, then 325 F. for 20 minutes.

Luncheon

MACARONI AND CHEESE*

GREEN SALAD

TEA

Macaroni and Cheese

    1 package macaroni
    4 quarts water
    2 cups light cream
    4 egg yolks
1½ cups coarsely-grated Cheddar cheese
    ½ cup bread crumbs
    1 teaspoon salt, pepper
    butter

Cook macaroni in water 5 minutes. Mix cream, egg yolks, cheese, salt, and pepper. Put layer of macaroni in buttered casserole and alternate with cheese mixture and macaroni. Sprinkle bread crumbs on top and dot with butter. Bake in 375 F. oven for 30 minutes.

Cauliflower Teapot—
Whieldon Type

57

Luncheon

```
LOBSTER STEW*
CRACKERS        DILL PICKLES
HONEYDEW MELON
POWDERED GINGER
COFFEE
```

Lobster Stew

    6 lobsters (1 to 1¼ lbs. each)
    2 cups salt water
    ¼ lb. butter
 1½ qts. milk
    1 pt. cream
    1 teaspoon paprika
    ½ teaspoon celery salt
    1 tablespoon Worcestershire sauce

Steam lobsters 15 minutes. Pick meat from shell and remove intestinal vein. Melt butter in large pan and add lobster meat and cook until lobster is well buttered. Add half of milk and cook over low heat, stirring constantly. Then add remainder of milk and bring to a boil. Add cream, half at a time, simmer a few minutes, then remove from fire and cool at least 12 hours. Reheat, season with paprika, celery salt, Worcestershire sauce and serve. Serves 4 to 6 persons.

Melon Tureen—
Strasbourg 1750-1770

Luncheon

```
LOBSTER TAIL SALAD*

GARLIC BREAD*

COFFEE
```

Lobster Tail Salad

    2 or 3 lobster tails
    1½ cups diced celery
    1 tablespoon minced onion
    ½ cup mayonnaise
    ½ cup sour cream
    1 teaspoon paprika
    1 tablespoon lemon juice

Boil lobster 10 or 15 minutes in salted water. Drain and cut lengthwise through center membrane and remove meat. Dice meat and chill, add celery and onion, and mix in mayonnaise, cream, paprika, and lemon juice.

Line salad bowl with greens and garnish with stuffed green olives.

Garlic Bread

    1 loaf French bread
    1 clove garlic mashed
    ⅛ lb. butter

Mash garlic and blend with butter. Slice loaf of bread keeping together at bottom of loaf. Butter bread with garlic butter and put in oven to heat thoroughly. Serve hot.

Luncheon

GNOCCHI*

WATERCRESS SALAD

STEWED FRUIT

TEA

Gnocchi

    1 cup water
    2 sprigs parsley
    3 slices onion
 1½ cups milk
    ¾ cup hominy (finest grind)
    6 tablespoons butter
    1 teaspoon salt
    ½ teaspoon pepper
    ¼ teaspoon nutmeg
    1 cup grated parmesan cheese

Boil water, parsley, and onion for 15 minutes. Strain and combine with milk and hominy and cook for 15 minutes. Remove from fire, add butter, salt, pepper, nutmeg, and half of cheese. Mix well and pour on buttered baking sheet to ½ inch thickness. When cold, cut in circles with cookie cutter and put in buttered casserole, each circle overlapping the other, and sprinkle with cheese and melted butter. Place in hot oven for 30 minutes.

Luncheon

SCALLOPED FISH*

STEWED TOMATOES

TEA

Scalloped Fish

    1 cup leftover fish
1½ cups white sauce
    1 tablespoon minced green pepper
    1 cup leftover vegetable
    ½ cup buttered bread crumbs

Mix fish, vegetable, and green pepper, and put in buttered casserole with bread crumbs on top. Bake at 375 F. for 30 minutes.

A Spanish Kitchen

Luncheon

CLAMS IN SHELLS*

GREEN SALAD

TEA

Clams in Shells

2 doz. clams
¼ lb. butter
1 onion sliced
¼ teaspoon pepper
coriander

Wash clams and put in casserole, shells and all. Dot with butter, slices of onion, freshly ground pepper and coriander. Cover and let cook 5 minutes in a moderate oven.

*Pineapple Teapot—
Whieldon Type*

Luncheon

CODFISH MEXICAN STYLE*

BOILED RICE

PERSIAN MELON BALLS*

COFFEE

Codfish Mexican Style
     1 package codfish
     1 cup olive oil
     5 tomatoes
     5 small potatoes
     5 hot red peppers
     ¼ cup green olives
     3 onions
     1 clove garlic

Soak codfish overnight in water. Cut in small squares. Grind and mash tomatoes, peppers, onions, and garlic, and fry in olive oil. Add codfish and peeled diced potatoes. Cook slowly until codfish is tender. Add sliced olives before removing from fire.

Persian Melon Balls
Serve Persian melon balls with chopped mint, lemon juice, and a few drops of almond extract.

Luncheon

Jellied Cucumber Ring with Crabmeat

1 package gelatine
4 tablespoons lemon juice
1¼ cups water
1 teaspoon grated onion
1 cup diced cucumber
paprika, pepper, and dill to taste
1½ cups crabmeat
⅓ cup French dressing
mayonnaise

Dissolve gelatine in water. Add lemon juice and seasonings, and chill until slightly thickened. Fold in cucumbers and chill in ring mold. Unmold on plate garnished
with lettuce. Fill ring with crabmeat mixed with French
dressing, and serve with mayonnaise.

Onion Cornbread

Use cornbread mix as directed, and pour in baking pan.
Peel and slice 2 onions. Sauté in butter and spread on
top of cornbread batter in pan. Bake 25 minutes.

Luncheon

CHEESE CORN PUDDING*

GREEN SALAD

TEA

Cheese Corn Pudding

- 2 cups fresh or canned corn
- ⅓ cup grated "store" cheese
- 3 tablespoons sugar
- 1 teaspoon cinnamon
- 3 eggs
- 3 tablespoons melted fat

Cut corn off cob and mix with cheese. Stir in sugar, cinnamon, beaten eggs, and melted fat. Line bottom of casserole with bread crumbs and pour in mixture. Bake in moderate oven (325 F.) for 40 minutes.

*Corn Pitcher—
American Pottery*

Luncheon

CRABMEAT CAKES*

GREEN SALAD

TEA

Crabmeat Cakes

    2 cups flaked crab meat
    1 cup thick white sauce
    salt, pepper
    1 teaspoon Worcestershire sauce
    1 teaspoon lemon juice
    1 egg, beaten
    bread crumbs

Mix fish with white sauce and seasoning. Shape in cakes, dip in bread crumbs, then in beaten egg, then roll in bread crumbs again and fry at 390 F. until brown. Mayonnaise may be substituted for white sauce.

Lettuce Head Dish—
19th Century
Staffordshire Pottery

Luncheon

LOBSTER PIE*

GREEN SALAD

TEA

Lobster Pie

2 lobsters
nutmeg, pepper, salt

Make in force-meat balls:
½ cup bread crumbs
1 teaspoon parsley
1 anchovy, mashed
1 teaspoon lemon peel, grated
mace, salt, pepper
1 egg yolk
2 tablespoons butter

pie crust
2 hard-cooked eggs
1 cup white sauce
½ cup white wine
1 tablespoon lemon juice

Boil lobster, cool, and remove meat. Season with salt
and pepper and nutmeg and put in pie pan on top of bottom pie crust. Make bread crumbs and seasoning into
force-meat balls and put on top of lobster. Add hard
cooked eggs, 1 cup white sauce, wine, lemon juice. Then
cover with pie crust and bake until crust is browned.

Luncheon

```
SPAGHETTI WITH CLAM
        SAUCE*
     GREEN SALAD
PRUNES WITH ALMOND
       FILLING*
        COFFEE
```

Spaghetti with Clam Sauce

Cook spaghetti in boiling water 12 to 15 minutes. Remove from water and drain. Make sauce of the following:

    2 cloves chopped garlic
    ¼ cup melted butter
    2 cups minced clams
    ½ cup chopped parsley
    salt, pepper
    1 cup clam juice
    ½ teaspoon Worcestershire sauce
    ½ teaspoon salt

Sauté garlic in 1 tablespoon butter. Add remaining butter, clams, clam juice, parsley, salt, pepper, etc. Serve over hot spaghetti with grated Parmesan cheese.

Prunes with Almond Filling

Soak dried prunes overnight in dry white wine. The next day simmer the prunes and wine until prunes are thoroughly tender. Remove pits and stuff with almond paste and pour wine residue over all. Serve with cream if desired.

Luncheon

FISH SOUFFLÉ*

LETTUCE AND TOMATO SALAD

TEA

Fish Soufflé

    2 cups cream of tomato soup
    3 eggs separated
    2 cups flaked fish
    ½ cup bread crumbs
    ½ teaspoon paprika
    1 tablespoon lemon juice
    salt, pepper, nutmeg

Mix tomato soup and beaten egg yolks, add fish, bread crumbs, and seasoning, and fold in stiffly beaten egg whites. Pour in buttered casserole, set in pan of hot water, and bake at 350 F. for 45 minutes. Serves 6.

A Swedish Kitchen

Luncheon

FINNAN HADDIE*

COLE SLAW

TEA

Finnan Haddie

    2 fillets of smoked finnan haddie
    1 onion, chopped
    1 green pepper, chopped
    2 tablespoons chopped parsley
    ¼ teaspoon paprika
    4 tablespoons butter
    1 cup light cream
    salt, pepper

Put finnan haddie in baking pan and dot with butter and sprinkle with chopped onion, green pepper, parsley, paprika, salt, and pepper. Pour cream over all and bake at 375 F. for 45 minutes. Baste frequently.

Carp-Fish Tureen—
Chelsea Porcelain

Luncheon

Cheese Rarebit

    1 lb. cheddar cheese
    2 tablespoons butter
    ½ teaspoon paprika
    ½ teaspoon dry mustard
    1 teaspoon Worcestershire sauce
    1 cup ale

Melt butter in double boiler, add cheese broken in small pieces. Mix seasoning with ale and add to cheese, stirring constantly. Cook until mixture bubbles and serve on toast.

Baked Bananas with Cranberry Sauce

    4 bananas
    1 can cranberry jelly

Cut bananas in half and put in buttered pan. Slice cranberry and put over bananas. Bake in slow oven (350 F.) for about 25 minutes. Serve hot with sauce.

Luncheon

> TUNA FISH À LA KING*
>
> GREEN SALAD
>
> ROSEMARY BISCUITS*
>
> TEA OR COFFEE

Tuna Fish à la King

    1 large can tuna fish
    3 tablespoons flour
    2 cups hot milk
    1 tablespoon Worcestershire sauce
    1 teaspoon chopped onion
    salt, pepper, cayenne
    3 tablespoons butter
    1 tablespoon diced green peppers
    1 tablespoon diced pimento

Melt butter, add peppers and onion. Sauté. Then add flour, seasonings, and milk, and cook until creamy, stirring constantly. Add pimentos and tuna fish, and serve on buttered toast garnished with parsley.

Rosemary Biscuits

Use Bisquick recipe and add ¼ cup chopped fresh rosemary leaves to bisquick flour. (If dried rosemary is used, soften leaves by soaking in hot milk.) Proceed with recipe as directed on package. Bake carefully and do not allow biscuits to get too hard.

Luncheon

Creamed Oysters

    1 quart oysters
    ½ cup heavy cream
    ¼ cup sherry wine
    ½ cup buttered bread crumbs
    celery salt, pepper

Heat cream in shallow casserole. Add sherry, then drained oysters. Season with celery salt and pepper, and cover top with buttered bread crumbs. Put under broiler for 5 minutes.

Cow Creamer—
Bennington Pottery

73

Luncheon

CHILI SHRIMPS*

MIXED GREEN SALAD

CUP CUSTARD

COFFEE

Chili Shrimps

2 lbs. raw shrimps
1 clove garlic, crushed
2 teaspoons chili powder
2 tablespoons butter
cream sauce

Cook shrimps 5 minutes, then shell and clean. Melt butter and add chili powder and crushed garlic and pour over shrimps. Let shrimps marinate in this sauce for 15 or 20 minutes. Make rich cream sauce and add shrimps and butter mixture. Serve with chopped parsley on top.

Covered Dish—
American Milk Glass

74

Luncheon

Scalloped Fish

2 lbs. fish boiled in water with:

| 3 or 4 bay leaves | 3 stalks celery |
| 1 onion | 1 carrot |

Bone fish. Butter baking dish and sprinkle with bread crumbs. Put in layers of fish alternating with bread crumbs. Put on one layer of grated almonds before the last layer of fish. Cover with hot tomato sauce and sprinkle bread crumbs on top. Bake 15 to 20 minutes at 350 F.

Finnish Cucumbers

2 large cucumbers	½ chopped dill or parsley
½ pt. sour cream	½ teaspoon celery seed
½ teaspoon freshly ground pepper	
garlic salt	

Pare cucumbers and slice very thin, salt, and drain. Put sour cream in bowl and add seasonings, mix and add cucumbers. Chill in refrigerator for two hours before serving.

Apple Snow

6 large apples	1 teaspoon lemon juice
3 egg whites	1 teaspoon grated nutmeg
¼ cup sugar	

Stew apples in a little water. Put through coarse sieve and set in ice box to cool. Beat whites of eggs to a froth and add sugar and lemon juice. Beat together with apples until thoroughly mixed. Set in ice box to cool. Serve with cream spiced with grated nutmeg.

75

Luncheon

Swiss Fondue

    2 cloves chopped garlic
1⅓ cups dry white wine
    ¾ cup Swiss cheese
    ⅓ cup milk
    salt, pepper, paprika
1½ tablespoons Kirsch
    1 tablespoon butter

Cook chopped garlic in dry white wine for 10 minutes. Strain. Cook Swiss cheese cut in small pieces with milk. Stir over slow fire until creamy. Then add salt, pepper, paprika, strained white wine, Kirsch, and butter. Serve on toast or French bread.

Green Herb Salad

Combination of Romaine and Boston lettuce, water cress, parsley, green peppers, cucumbers, and fresh basil. Serve with French dressing.

Pie dish—
Connecticut Sliped
Decorated Ware

Part Three

Dinner

```
ONION SOUP
FRENCH FRIED SHRIMPS*
COCKTAIL SAUCE*
LETTUCE AND TOMATO SALAD
ICE CREAM WITH MARRONS
COFFEE
```

French Fried Shrimp

- 2 lbs. shrimp
- 2 eggs
- 2 tablespoons milk
- ½ cup bread crumbs
- ½ cup flour
- 4 tablespoons paprika
- ¾ teaspoon salt
- ¾ teaspoon pepper

Remove shrimp from shell and take out black vein. Beat eggs, add milk. Mix bread crumbs, flour, and seasoning. Dip shrimp in egg mixture. Fry in deep fat until golden brown. Serve with cocktail sauce.

Cocktail Sauce

Combine the following:

- 1 cup mayonnaise
- 4 tablespoons chili sauce
- 1 teaspoon horseradish
- 1 teaspoon Worcestershire sauce
- 1 tablespoon vinegar
- juice of ½ clove garlic

Dinner

```
GRILLED MUSHROOMS ON TOAST
        BAKED BASS*
  BROCCOLI-CHEESE CASSEROLE
      PRUNE WHIP WITH
    BLANCHED ALMONDS*
          COFFEE
```

Baked Bass aux Fines Herbes

    4 lb. bass
    1 tablespoon lemon juice
    salt, pepper
    1 onion
    ⅓ cup butter

Wash and dry bass. Rub with mixture of salt, freshly ground pepper, and lemon juice. Place fish in baking pan. Make incisions in skin and put thin slices of onion in incisions. Pour ⅓ cup melted butter over fish and baste frequently. Put on hot platter and serve with Herb Sauce (see recipe on page 26).

Prune Whip with Blanched Almonds

    1 lb. stewed prunes put through sieve
    3 egg whites
    juice of lemon
    ½ cup sugar
    ½ cup sliced blanched almonds

Beat egg whites stiff and add to prunes, add sugar, lemon juice, and almonds. Bake about 20 minutes in 325 F. oven. Serve cold with whipped cream.

Dinner

VEGETABLE SOUP
BROILED FILET OF SOLE
PEAS   RICE WITH SAFFRON*
STRAWBERRY WHIP*
COFFEE

Rice with Saffron

½ lb. rice
2 tablespoons butter
1 pt. chicken broth
3 onions sliced
3 tomatoes (cut fine)
1 pinch saffron

Wash and drain rice. Put Crisco in pan and sauté onions and tomatoes. Then add broth and rice, and cook over slow fire until rice is done (35 to 45 minutes). When nearly done, add saffron.

Strawberry Whip

1 cup sieved strawberries
3 egg whites
¼ cup sugar

Beat egg whites until stiff, then add sugar and strawberries, beating continually. Chill and serve cold, or pour into baking dish and bake at 375 F. for 30 minutes.

Pea-in-Pod—
Chelsea Porcelain

Dinner

```
AVOCADO COCKTAIL
BROILED SWORDFISH*
RICE WITH PEAS AND CARROTS*
PERSIAN MELON SLICES
WITH SHERRY
COFFEE
```

Broiled Swordfish

    2 lbs. swordfish
    1 tablespoon lemon juice
    6 tablespoons butter
    salt, pepper

Wash fish and wipe dry. Sprinkle with lemon juice, salt, and pepper and spread with butter. Broil at 550 F. for 3 minutes. Turn and spread with remaining butter and cook until brown. Serve with parsley and melted butter.

Rice with Peas and Carrots

    1 cup of rice
    1¼ cup water
    1 clove garlic
    2 tablespoons butter
    1 cup peas and diced carrots mixed

Wash rice and put in saucepan with water and garlic. When it begins to boil, turn to slow heat and cook 1 hour. Then add salt, pepper, butter, diced carrots, and peas.

Dinner

BORSCHT*
BROILED POMPANO*
STRING BEANS
BAKED FRUIT COMPOTE*
COFFEE

Borscht

2 cans consomme
1 jar "Junior Foods" pureed beets
2 teaspoons scraped onion
2 teaspoons lemon juice

May be frozen as jellied soup or served hot topped with sour cream.

Broiled Pompano

3 lb. pompano
6 tablespoons butter
2 tablespoons lemon juice
1 tablespoon chopped parsley
salt, pepper, thyme, marjoram

Clean fish, sprinkle with lemon and rub with butter mixed with salt, pepper, thyme, marjoram. Place fish on sheet and put under broiler and broil at 550 F. for 10 minutes. Turn fish and brown on top side. Serve with remaining seasoned melted butter; lemon slices and parsley.

Baked Fruit Compote

Use fresh or canned assorted fruits, such as peaches, pears, apricots, cherries and pineapple. Arrange fruit in layers in casserole and sprinkle each layer with brown sugar and dot with butter and blanched almonds. Cover top with macaroon crumbs moistened with Grand Marnier. Bake 15 or 20 minutes. Serve hot with cream.

Dinner

AVOCADO-GRAPEFRUIT COCKTAIL
TROUT MEUNIÈRE*
CARROT BALLS*
CREAMED NEW POTATOES
SPANISH CREAM
COFFEE

Trout Meunière

Season trout with salt and pepper. Dip in milk and flour and sauté in olive oil until brown. Remove fish, drain oil, and put 1 tablespoon of garlic butter in pan for each serving. Brown butter and pour over fish together with chopped parsley and lemon juice.

Carrot Balls

    2 cups mashed carrots
    2 eggs
    2 tablespoons flour
    1 tablespoon butter
    ½ teaspoon salt

Cook carrots, drain dry, and mash. Add 2 beaten eggs, flour, and melted butter. (If you have not drained carrots carefully you will need to add more flour.) Shape into balls about 1" in diameter and fry in deep fat. Serve with a sprig of parsley.

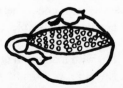

Pomegranite Dish—
Meissen Porcelain

84

Dinner

CONSOMME
POTAGE ROYALE*
PEAS   SMALL WHOLE BEETS
GREEN SALAD CHUTNEY DRESSING*
PINEAPPLE SLICES IN KIRSCH
COFFEE

Potage Royale

1 can tomato sauce with:
   1 sprig thyme
   ½ onion sautéed

Poulette sauce made of:
   2 tablespoons butter
   1 tablespoon flour
   1 cup cream
   4 egg yolks
   paprika, salt, lemon juice
   ¼ cup white wine

Blend the two sauces and add:
   1 pt. small oysters
   1 pt. crab meat
   1 pt. lobster meat
   1 cup shrimps

Put in casserole and grate cheese over top and bake in oven until brown at 350 F.

Chutney Salad Dressing

   ½ teaspoon salt
   ¼ teaspoon ground pepper
   2 tablespoons terragon vinegar
   5 tablespoons olive oil
   2 tablespoons chutney

Beat with an egg beater. When thick, add chutney.

Dinner

```
ICED·CURRY SOUP*
CRABMEAT CASSEROLE*
ROMAINE LETTUCE
WITH WEST INDIES DRESSING (see page 32)
FRUIT COMPOTE
```

Iced Curry Soup

1 can green pea soup
1 can beef consomme
½ can tomato madrilene
1¼ cups light cream
juice of 1½ lemons
salt, pepper
1½ tablespoons curry

Combine soups and cream and heat over low fire stirring constantly. Add salt, pepper, curry, and lemon juice. Cool and chill in ice box. Garnish with chopped parsley.

Crabmeat Casserole

2 cups fresh crabmeat
½ cup bread crumbs
¼ cup light cream
3 tablespoons melted butter
1 tablespoon lemon juice
1 tablespoon Worcestershire sauce
4 tablespoons catsup
¼ teaspoon dry mustard
salt, pepper
½ cup grated Swiss cheese

Mix crabmeat with other ingredients and put in casserole. Sprinkle top with layer of grated Swiss cheese and dot with butter. Bake in moderate oven (350 F.) for about 20 minutes.

Dinner

```
BROILED FLOUNDER FILLETS*
STEWED TOMATOES
MASHED POTATOES
FRESH FRUIT
COFFEE
```

Broiled Flounder Fillets

2 lbs. flounder fillets
1 tablespoon lemon juice
1 tablespoon chopped onion
6 tablespoons melted butter
2 teaspoons paprika
¼ teaspoon thyme
salt, pepper

Wash fish and rub with lemon juice. Place fish on aluminum foil and sprinkle with mixed butter and seasonings. Broil at 500 F. for 5 minutes, then turn, sprinkle with remaining butter sauce, and broil 5 minutes more. Serve with lemon slices and parsley.

*Dish with Grapes—
Delft Pottery*

87

Dinner

```
HALIBUT BAKED WITH
TOMATO SOUP*
SCALLOPED POTATOES—HERBS*
GREEN SALAD
FLOATING ISLAND PUDDING
COFFEE
```

Halibut Baked with Tomato Soup

    2 lbs. sliced halibut
    1 large onion, sliced
    4 tablespoons butter
    2 tablespoons flour
    salt, pepper
    1 tablespoon tarragon vinegar
    1 can cream of tomato soup

Put two tablespoons of butter and half of onion slices into bottom of baking pan. Season fish with salt and pepper and dredge with flour. Lay fish in baking pan. Put remainder of onion slices on fish and dot with remainder of butter. Pour about ½ inch water mixed with tarragon vinegar over fish, and bake in hot oven (350 F.) for 30 minutes. Pour tomato soup over fish and cook about 10 minutes longer.

Scalloped Potatoes with Herbs

    4 medium potatoes
    1 cup diced celery
    ¼ cup chopped chives, thyme, parsley, and marjoram
    ¼ cup butter
    1 cup milk

Butter a Pyrex baking dish. Put in a layer of peeled, thin-sliced raw potatoes and a layer of diced celery. Chop fine the chives, thyme, parsley, and marjoram. Mix with butter. Dot layer of potatoes and celery with herb butter. Add another layer of potatoes and celery with herb butter and continue until dish is full. Pour milk over all and top with a layer of buttered bread crumbs. Bake at 350 F. for about 40 minutes.

An Italian Kitchen

Dinner

```
TOMATO JUICE COCKTAIL
BROILED SALMON STEAKS*
PEAS        NEW POTATOES*
FRESH GRAPES
CHEESE AND CRACKERS
COFFEE
```

Broiled Salmon Steaks

    2 lbs. salmon steaks
    juice of 1 lemon
    4 tablespoons butter
    salt, pepper

Wash fish and wipe dry. Sprinkle with lemon juice and let stand 10 minutes. Dust fish with flour, salt, and pepper. Set broiler at 500 F. and place fish on aluminum foil 3 inches below flame. Brush with butter and lemon juice. Broil 3 minutes, turn, brush with butter and lemon juice, and broil 5 minutes. Serve with parsley and lemon slices.

New Potatoes

Serve with 2 tablespoons melted butter, 2 tablespoons chopped parsley, and 1 tablespoon chopped chives.

Dinner

FROZEN TOMATO COCKTAIL*
BAKED SOLE WITH HERBS*
PEAS   MASHED POTATOES
CHERRY JELLO WITH FRUIT
AND NUTS
COFFEE

Frozen Tomato Cocktail

7 large tomatoes
1 small white onion
1 teaspoon salt
¼ teaspoon freshly
   ground black pepper
1 teaspoon lemon juice
Sauce:

     5 tablespoons mayonnaise
     1 tablespoon minced parsley
     1 teaspoon curry powder

Scald and skin tomatoes and chop fine. Peel and grate onion. Add seasoning and chill in freezing tray of refrigerator until half frozen. Mix mayonnaise, parsley, and curry powder and serve on top of tomato in cocktail glasses.

Baked Sole with Herbs

6 fillets of sole   1 bay leaf
1½ tablespoons onion   1 sprig thyme
1 teaspoon lemon juice 1 tablespoon chopped parsley
½ cup white wine

Wash and dry sole and put in baking dish. Sprinkle with lemon juice and onion and pour on wine. Add bay leaf, thyme, and parsley. Cover fish and cook in moderate oven (350 F.) for 10 minutes. Remove cover and glaze under broiler. Serve with liquid in pan, adding more wine or cream if desired.

Dinner

```
CREAM OF TOMATO SOUP
BROILED LOBSTER*
MIXED GREEN SALAD
BAKED PINEAPPLE* WITH
CUSTARD SAUCE*
COFFEE
```

Broiled Lobster

Place lobster on its back and cut lengthwise from mouth to tail. Open and remove stomach and intestine. Crack the claws.

Put the lobster on the broiler rack and cover with bread crumbs, butter, and paprika. Broil close to heat 5 minutes. Baste with butter and serve with melted hot butter and slices of lemon.

Baked Pineapple

Cut the pineapple in half and remove the meat. Cut meat in small pieces and mix with 1 cup granulated sugar. Put mixture back in pineapple. Dot with butter and put halves together and put in oven. Bake at 375 F. for 30 minutes. Serve hot with custard sauce.

Custard Sauce

        1 cup milk
        2 egg yolks
        2 tablespoons sugar
        ¼ teaspoon salt
        1 teaspoon vanilla

Scald milk in double boiler. Pour over beaten eggs, sugar, and salt and return to double boiler and cook until it thickens, stirring constantly. Add vanilla.

Dinner

SHAD ROE WITH OYSTERS*
SCALLOPED TOMATOES
FRENCH FRIED POTATOES
JELLIED PEARS*
COFFEE

Shad Roe with Oysters

    3 shad roes
    ½ lb. butter
    salt, pepper
    2 doz. oysters
    2 eggs
    1 cup cracker crumbs
    cooking fat

Sauté roe in butter 15 or 20 minutes. Dip oysters in egg and cracker crumbs and fry in deep fat. Serve roes on platter and sprinkle with melted butter, chopped parsley, chopped chives, chervil, and lemon wedges. Arrange oysters on platter around roes.

Jellied Pears

    6 large pears
    sugar syrup
    1 pt. claret
    1 stick cinnamon
    1 teaspoon lemon juice
    1 teaspoon vanilla
    1½ teaspoons gelatine

Boil pears in mixture of sugar syrup, claret, etc., until tender. Remove pears and mix remaining syrup with gelatine dissolved in cold water. Pour over pears and set in ice box to cool and thicken. Serve with cream.

Dinner

```
CREAM OF ASPARAGUS SOUP
        FISH CURRY*
PEAS      SMALL WHOLE BEETS
      HONEY DEW MELON
           COFFEE
```

Fish Curry

     2 lbs. codfish, haddock, or halibut
 1½ cups water
     1 tablespoon curry powder
     1 bay leaf
     1 shallot, .chopped
     2 medium sized onions, chopped
 ¼ lb. butter
     1 tablespoon chopped parsley
     salt, cayenne

Cook fish in water with curry powder and bay leaf for 15 minutes. Meanwhile put butter in pan and sauté chopped shallot, onions, and parsley. When browned, add fish, salt, and cayenne and continue to cook until seasoning has penetrated fish and fish is tender. Serve with lemon slices.

Melon Dish—
French Porcelain

Dinner

```
GREEN PEA—CHICKEN SOUP
(mix 1 can of each)
GRILLED SWORDFISH*
STRING BEANS    CAULIFLOWER
LEMON PUDDING*
COFFEE
```

Grilled Swordfish

　　2 swordfish steaks
　　1 cup sliced onions
　　½ cup olive oil
　　2 tablespoons water
　　2 teaspoons chopped parsley
　　paprika, salt and pepper
　　4 bay leaves

Pierce swordfish with bay leaves and marinate for 1 hour in mixture of sliced onion, olive oil, parsley and spices. Broil fish until done, basting frequently with onion mixture and serve with residue of mixture as sauce.

Lemon Pudding

　　1 cup sugar
　　4 tablespoons flour
　　2 tablespoons butter
　　¼ teaspoon salt
　　5 tablespoons lemon juice
　　grated rind of 1 lemon
　　1½ cups milk
　　3 eggs separated

Mix first four ingredients together thoroughly. Add lemon juice and rind. Add milk slowly, then egg yolks. Lastly, stiffly beaten egg whites. Pour into buttered baking dish. Set in pan of hot water and bake in a slow oven (325 F.) for 45 minutes.

Dinner

```
CREAM OF MUSHROOM SOUP
BAKED ROCK FISH*
BAKED CABBAGE*
ORANGES WITH
COCONUT-MACAROONS
COFFEE
```

Baked Rock Fish

    4 lbs. rock fish
    3 potatoes
    2 carrots
    2 onions
    ½ green pepper
    1 cup water

Season fish with salt and pepper and put in a greased pan. Slice potatoes, carrots, onions, and pepper, and put in pan with fish. Pour water over all and bake in 350 F. oven for 1¼ hours, basting frequently with mixture of:

    ¼ cup olive oil
    1 teaspoon creole powder
    juice of ½ lemon

Add enough water to have 1 cup sauce left to serve with fish.

Baked Cabbage

    2 cups boiled cabbage
    1 cup cream sauce
    ½ cup grated cheese
    bread crumbs

Put cabbage in buttered baking dish in layers with cream sauce and cheese. Cover top with bread crumbs, dot with butter, and brown in oven 15 or 20 minutes.

Dinner

TOMATO JUICE COCKTAIL

BAKED SLICED COD*

CHEESE AND SPINACH*

BAVARIAN CREAM

COFFEE

Baked Sliced Cod

4 thick slices fresh cod
2 tablespoons butter
1 tablespoon catsup
1 tablespoon Worcestershire sauce
¼ cup milk
2 tablespoons chopped parsley

Season fish slices with salt and pepper and sprinkle with flour. Butter a baking pan and put fish in. Dot fish with butter and pour on mixture of catsup, Worcestershire sauce, parsley, and milk. Bake at 350 F. for 25 minutes, basting several times.

Cheese and Spinach

2 lbs. spinach
1 cup grated cheese
¼ cup bread crumbs
2 tablespoons melted butter
1 egg

Cook spinach, chop and put through sieve. Add grated cheese, melted butter, bread crumbs, and beaten egg. Put in buttered baking dish and bake in moderate oven (350 F.) for 20 minutes.

Dinner

```
BLACK BEAN SOUP
POMPANO IN PAPER*
EGGPLANT-TOMATO CASSEROLE*
BOILED POTATOES FINES HERBES*
ORANGE ICE WITH MARMALADE
COFFEE
```

Pompano in Paper

    1 pompano
    ⅛ lb. butter
    2 tablespoons minced parsley
    2 slices lemon
    salt, pepper, paprika, garlic

Dry fish, season with salt, pepper, paprika, and garlic. Brush with oil and brown quickly under broiler. Mix butter and minced parsley. Oil a sheet of brown paper. Lay fish on it and spread parsley and butter on fish with lemon. Fold paper around fish and twist ends. Put in oiled pan and bake about 15 minutes in moderate oven. Serve in papers and garnish with lemon, watercress, and extra parsley butter.

Eggplant and Tomato Casserole

    1 large eggplant, peeled and sliced
    1 can solid pack tomatoes
    1 green pepper, sliced
    3 medium sized onions
    salt, pepper, dash of nutmeg

Sauté eggplant, green pepper, and onions. Arrange in layers in buttered casserole, alternating a layer of eggplant, pepper, and onions with a layer of tomatoes. Put buttered bread crumbs on top and bake in 400 F. oven 30 minutes.

Boiled Potatoes—Fines Herbes

Peel and boil small potatoes. Serve with melted butter, 1 teaspoon chopped parsley, 1 teaspoon chopped chives.

Dinner

```
TOMATO JUICE
SMELTS BERNAISE*
SPINACH GERMAN STYLE*
BAKED POTATOES
STRAWBERRIES WITH KIRSCH*
COFFEE
```

Smelts Bernaise

Split smelts and remove bones. Rub with olive oil, lemon, salt, and pepper. Broil in broiler 2 minutes on each side. Serve with Bernaise sauce.

Spinach German Style

    2 lbs. spinach
    1 tablespoon flour
    1 tablespoon grated onion
    2 tablespoons butter
    1 cup beef consomme or beef bouillon
    ginger, salt, pepper

Boil spinach in salt water. Drain and mash fine. Brown flour and grated onion in butter. Add beef consomme or beef bouillon. Season with ginger, salt, and pepper. Mix in spinach and serve hot.

Strawberries with Kirsch

Sprinkle strawberries with powdered sugar and 1 tablespoon of Kirsch and set in ice box. Whip heavy cream and flavor with 1 teaspoon Kirsch. Mix with strawberries and serve.

Dinner

```
BAKED ROCK COD*
BRAISED ONIONS*
BAKED POTATOES
MELON SLICES WITH GRAPES*
COFFEE
```

Baked Rock Cod

1 rock cod	⅛ teaspoon basil
1 bay leaf	salt and pepper
1 clove garlic on toothpick	3 tablespoons butter
⅛ teaspoon oregano	

Mix seasonings with butter and stuff fish. Add garlic on toothpick, wrap fish in oiled paper and put in pan and bake in moderate oven for 30 minutes. Remove garlic and serve with horseradish sauce (see recipe on page 26).

Braised Onions

1 lb. small white onions
1 cup beef broth
1 tablespoon butter

Cook onions in boiling water 15 minutes. Drain and put in buttered casserole. Pour broth over onions and sprinkle with sugar and dot with remaining butter. Bake in moderate oven until soft.

Melon Slices with Grapes

Quarter a Persian melon and pile on white grapes which have been seasoned with confectioners sugar and finely chopped fresh mint, about 2 tablespoons to a melon section.

Dinner

```
BAKED BLUEFISH*
SAVORY STRING BEANS*
MASHED POTATOES
VANILLA ICE CREAM WITH
BAR-LE-DUC
COFFEE
```

Baked Bluefish

3 lbs. bluefish
salt, pepper, paprika, lemon juice
2 tablespoons butter
1 tablespoon parsley
1 tablespoon chives

Split the fish and place in well buttered baking dish. Sprinkle with salt, pepper, paprika, and lemon juice. Cream butter with parsley and chives, and spread on fish. Cook about 25 minutes, basting frequently. Serve with sprigs of parsley and lemon slices.

Savory String Beans

2 medium sized onions
2 tablespoons butter
2 cups tomato juice
2 cloves
salt, pepper
1 tablespoon chopped parsley

Chop the onions and sauté in butter. Add the string beans, cut French style. Add tomato juice and seasonings, and cook until beans are tender. Add 1 tablespoon butter, chopped parsley, and serve.

Dinner

HOT TOMATO MADRILENE
STUFFED FLOUNDER*
NEW POTATOES   PEAS
GREEN SALAD
PERSIAN MELON BALLS*
COFFEE

Stuffed Flounder

    small whole flounders
    ¼ cup fresh crabmeat to each fish
    1 tablespoon butter
    1 teaspoon sherry wine
    lemon slices, parsley

Remove bones from small whole flounders. Sauté crabmeat, ¼ cup to each fish, in butter and sherry wine. Stuff flounder with crabmeat and broil until brown and tender. Serve with lemon slices and parsley.

Persian Melon Balls

Scoop out balls from melon. Sprinkle with powdered sugar, lime juice, chopped fresh mint, and a few drops of almond extract. Return to melon shell, chill, and serve.

*Squash Tureen—
South of France Faience*

Dinner

Baked Halibut

    3 lbs. halibut steaks
    ⅓ cup butter
    ¾ cup chopped onions
    1 bay leaf
    ¼ teaspoon thyme
    1 clove minced garlic

Sprinkle halibut with salt and pepper and dot with butter. Butter baking dish generously and put in chopped onions, garlic, bay leaf, and thyme. Put halibut on top of this, and cover with buttered paper and bake at 350 F. for 25 or 30 minutes, basting often. Remove fish to platter and serve with butter left in baking dish. Sprinkle with parsley and serve with lemon slices.

Minted Peaches

    6 fresh peaches (or container of frozen peaches)
    3 tablespoons green creme de menthe
    2 tablespoons powdered sugar
    ½ pt. heavy cream
    6 sprigs fresh mint

Whip cream and add creme de menthe. Set in ice box for about 1 hour. Slice peaches and mix with sugar. To serve, mix whipped minted cream and peaches, and serve with sprig of mint on top.

Dinner

```
BOILED PERCH*
PEAS
CREAMED NEW POTATOES
MARMALADE APPLE PIE*
COFFEE
```

Boiled Perch

    2 lb. perch
    1 cup water
    1 cup white wine
    bay leaf, clove garlic
    anchovy butter
    6 sprigs parsley
    2 scallions
    2 cloves
    salt, pepper

Clean and wash fish. Put water and wine in kettle and bring to a boil. Then add bay leaf, garlic, parsley, scallions, and cloves. Boil 10 minutes. Put fish in kettle and boil 10 or 15 minutes. Serve with balls of anchovy butter and slices of lemon.

Marmalade Apple Pie

    pie crust
    4 or 5 apples, pared and sliced
    2 tablespoons brown sugar
    1 teaspoon ginger
    1 teaspoon lemon peel, grated
    lemon or orange marmalade

Put bottom crust in pie plate. Alternate layers of sugar mixed with ginger, and lemon peel and apples. Spread thin layer of lemon or orange marmalade (about 2 tablespoons) on top before putting on top crust. Bake in a moderate oven until apples are tender.

Dinner

HADDOCK AU GRATIN*

PEAS   SAUTÉED CUCUMBERS*

FRESH CHERRIES IN GLASS
BOWL WITH ICE CUBES

COFFEE

Haddock au Gratin

    2 lbs. haddock
    bay leaf, thyme, salt, pepper
    1 can corn (cream style)
    1 cup rich cream sauce
    ½ cup grated cheese

Cook fish in enough water to cover, with bay leaf, thyme, salt, and pepper for about 10 minutes. Remove from fire, cool, and flake. Mix corn with fish and put in casserole in layers with cream sauce. Sprinkle grated cheese on top and brown in oven about 20 minutes (350 F.).

Sautéed Cucumbers

Cut cucumbers 1 inch thick and roll in mashed corn flakes, then sauté in butter for 20 minutes.

*Fish Pickle Dish—
American Milk Glass*

Dinner

CREAM OF CORN SOUP

SHRIMP GUMBO*

MIXED GREEN SALAD

MARSHMALLOW PEACH CUSTARD*

COFFEE

Shrimp Gumbo

2 lbs. raw shrimp
2 tablespoons butter or bacon fat
2 tablespoons flour
2 cups water
1 cup tomatoes (canned)
1 cup sliced okra (canned)
½ cup chopped celery
¼ cup chopped green pepper
¼ cup chopped onion
1 clove garlic, chopped
1 red pepper (whole)
salt, pepper
¼ teaspoon marjoram, pinch of thyme, pinch of sage, and several drops Tabasco sauce
2 cups boiled rice

In an iron pot melt butter and stir in flour, then add water to make gravy. Add one cup canned tomatoes. Sauté in butter the sliced okra and add to pot. Also add celery, green pepper, onion, garlic, red pepper, salt and pepper. Add cleaned raw shrimp and enough water to cover. Simmer 1 hour. Remove red pepper, add marjoram, thyme, and sage, and simmer another 30 minutes. Serve with steamed rice.

Marshmallow Peach Custard

    1 cup milk
    1 cup canned or frozen peach juice
    1 teaspoon grated lemon rind
    2 tablespoons sugar
    3 tablespoons cornstarch
    1 egg
    1 doz. marshmallows
    ¼ teaspoon lemon extract
    6 peach halves or 1 package frozen peaches

Combine milk, peach juice, sugar, and lemon rind, and put in double boiler. Add cornstarch and stir until thick, and cook 25 minutes. Add beaten egg and marshmallows and cook 5 minutes longer. Add flavoring and pour into mold or individual dishes, arranging peaches on top of custard.

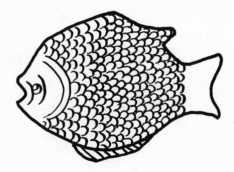

Fish Platter—
American Milk Glass

Dinner

```
BRUSSELS SPROUTS SOUP*
BROILED SCALLOPS*
STRING BEANS
FRENCH BREAD PUDDING*
COFFEE
```

Brussels Sprouts Soup

    1 pt. Brussels sprouts
    Bouquet of:
        1 bay leaf
        3 sprigs parsley
        3 slices onion
        1 whole clove
    1 can chicken broth
    ½ cup light cream

Cook brussels sprouts in salted water and bouquet of seasoning, drain and put through sieve. Season with salt, pepper, and nutmeg, add broth and bring to boil, and add ½ cup light cream.

Broiled Scallops

    1 pt. scallops
    4 tablespoons butter or margarine
    celery salt, pepper
    1 tablespoon lemon juice

Put scallops in shallow baking pan. Sprinkle with celery salt, freshly ground pepper, and lemon juice. Pour melted butter over scallops and broil 5 minutes. Turn to brown on all sides and broil about 8 minutes longer. Serve with slices of lemon and cucumber.

French Bread Pudding

- 2 cups milk
- 3 tablespoons sugar
- ½ loaf stale French bread
- 2 tablespoons seedless raisins
- 1 tablespoon sliced candied orange peel
- 2 beaten eggs

Put milk and sugar in double boiler, bring to boil, and pour over bread. Cover and let steep for 15 minutes. Mash bread with a fork and add raisins, orange peel, and eggs. Stir until well blended. Put in buttered mold and bake in a slow oven 45 minutes. Unmold and serve with cream.

A Normandy Kitchen

Dinner

```
TOMATO MADRILENE AND
PEA SOUP MIXED
SHRIMP SAUTÉ*
STRING BEANS—LIMA BEANS
MARMALADE BREAD PUDDING*
COFFEE
```

Shrimp Sauté

    2 lbs. cleaned raw shrimps
    ¼ lb. butter
    4 tablespoons parsley
    ¼ teaspoon curry
    ⅛ teaspoon garlic salt
    pepper

Put butter and seasoning in saucepan. Add chopped parsley and shrimp, and sauté about 5 minutes. Put shrimp on toast squares and pour on butter and parsley sauce. Sprinkle with lemon juice. Serve with lemon slices.

String Beans and Lima Beans

Use equal quantity of string beans and lima beans. Season with butter, salt, pepper, and nutmeg.

Marmalade Bread Pudding

    3 egg yolks
    1 cup grated bread crumbs
    ¾ cup orange or apricot marmalade
    3 tablespoons sugar
    3 tablespoons melted butter

Mix ingredients thoroughly and steam in covered mold 1½ hours. Serve hot with whipped cream.

Dinner

```
TOMATO JUICE
BAKED WHITEFISH*
BROCCOLI WITH
HOLLANDAISE SAUCE
FRUIT TAPIOCA CREAM*
COFFEE
```

Baked Whitefish

    3 lb. whitefish
    1 sliced onion
    1 tablespoon chopped parsley
    4 tablespoons butter
    ¾ cup white wine
    ¼ cup bread crumbs

Place fish in buttered baking dish. Cover with onion, parsley, butter, and wine. Sprinkle with salt and pepper and bread crumbs, dot with butter, and bake in 350 F. oven for 35 minutes.

Fruit Tapioca Cream

    ¼ cup tapioca
    2 cups milk
    2 eggs, separated
    1 package frozen strawberries or peaches

Cook milk and tapioca in double boiler until tapioca is transparent. Beat egg yolks and add. Cook until thickened. Remove and fold in beaten egg whites and defrosted fruit. Pour into molds and cool. Serve with cream.

*Pie Dish—
German Fayencen*

Dinner

GREEN PEA SOUP
LOBSTER SAVANNAH*
GREEN SALAD WITH FRESH
BASIL LEAVES
LEMON FRENCH DRESSING
FRUIT TARTE   COFFEE

Lobster Savannah

1 large boiled lobster
½ lb. mushrooms, sliced
2 tablespoons red and green peppers, sliced
salt, pepper, paprika, garlic
¼ cup sherry wine
¾ cup heavy cream
2 egg yolks
grated Parmesan cheese

Cut boiled lobster up back from top to bottom. Remove meat from body and claws and cut into cubes. Sauté in butter the mushrooms, red and green pepper slices, salt, pepper, paprika, and garlic. Add sherry wine. Mix heavy cream with yolks of eggs and add to the mushroom mixture. Put in lobster meat and stir over hot fire. Fill lobster shell with finished mixture, cover with grated Parmesan cheese, and put in hot oven 5 to 10 minutes. Bake to golden brown.

Dinner

CLAM AND TOMATO BOUILLON
(1 can of each)
BROILED MACKEREL*
SPINACH RING WITH
CREAMED MUSHROOMS*
FROZEN CHEESE CAKE   COFFEE

Broiled Mackerel-Onion Butter

2 lb. mackerel	onion butter:
(or small mackerels)	3 tablespoons butter
juice of 1 lemon	1 teaspoon mustard
salt and pepper	1 teaspoon lemon juice
flour butter	1 tablespoon minced onion
	½ clove minced garlic

Split fish open, sprinkle with salt, pepper, and lemon juice, and let stand for 10 minutes. Then rub fish with butter, place on paper, and broil for 5 minutes. Spread onion butter on fish and broil about 3 minutes. White fish, bonito, bass, bluefish or perch may be broiled the same way.

Spinach Ring with Creamed Mushrooms

2 cups cooked spinach	1 lb. mushrooms,
3 eggs, beaten	sliced and boiled
2 tablespoons butter	cream sauce
½ cup milk	
1 tablespoon flour	
salt, pepper, nutmeg	

Melt butter, add flour, then add milk, stirring until it thickens. Add beaten egg yolks, then spinach chopped fine. Beat egg whites and fold in together with seasoning. Pour in greased ring, mold, set in hot water, and bake in moderate oven (350 F.) for 35 to 40 minutes. Empty mold on platter and serve with creamed mushrooms in center.

Dinner

FRIED SHAD ROE

PEAS   CARROT SOUFFLÉ*

ROMAN PUNCH À LA
CASTLE GARDEN*

COFFEE

Fried Shad Roe

> 2 lbs. shad roe
> 3 tablespoons lemon juice
> salt, pepper
> ¼ lb. butter
> 2 eggs, beaten
> ¾ cup cracker crumbs
> 1 tablespoon chopped parsley

Sprinkle roe with lemon juice, salt, and pepper. Dip in cracker, egg, then cracker crumbs. Melt butter in frying pan and add roe. Brown on one side then turn. Cook about 10 minutes. Serve with the butter it was cooked in and chopped parsley and lemon slices.

Carrot Soufflé

> 1 cup sieved carrots
> 2 cups white sauce
> 3 eggs, separated
> 1 teaspoon chopped onion
> salt, pepper

Beat egg yolks and mix with white sauce. Add carrots and chopped onion. Fold in stiffly beaten egg whites. Put in buttered ring baking dish. Set in pan of water and bake in moderate over (375 F.) for 45 minutes. Serve with buttered peas in center.

See opposite page for Roman Punch à la Castle Garden

Dinner

Scalloped Oysters

    2 doz. oysters in liquor
    1½ cups salted cracker crumbs
    ½ cup melted butter
    1 cup canned mushroom soup
    ½ cup oyster liquor

Drain oysters and reserve liquor. In buttered casserole put layer of cracker crumbs, then layer of oysters. Dot each layer with butter and sprinkle with salt and pepper. Mix mushroom soup with oyster liquor and pour over all. Sprinkle top with cracker crumbs and dot with butter. Bake at 375 F. for 20 minutes.

Roman Punch à la Castle Garden

(Served at Castle Garden in 1848 and taken from record book.)

    1 qt. water
    1 lb. sugar
    2 lemons
    3 cups rum and ½ cup brandy mixed
Strain through sieve and freeze.

Note: This recipe is adapted from one in an original manuscript, through the courtesy of the New York Historical Society.

115

Dinner

Fried Frogs Legs

10 pairs frogs legs	salt, pepper
juice ½ lemon	1 clove garlic
milk	½ lb. butter
flour	

Sprinkle frogs legs with lemon and let stand 10 minutes. Place in saucepan and cover with milk and let stand another 10 minutes. Drain; season with salt and pepper and dredge with flour. Crush clove of garlic in butter. Melt butter and fry frogs legs until brown. Serve with tartar sauce.

Orange Bavarian Cream

½ tablespoon gelatine	¼ teaspoon salt
¼ cup cold water	1 pt. heavy cream
1 cup orange juice	1 teaspoon vanilla
⅓ cup sugar	

Soak gelatine in water and dissolve in heated orange juice. Add sugar and salt. Set bowl in cold water and stir until it begins to thicken. Add cream whipped stiff and vanilla. Pour into mold to chill. Serve garnished with orange sections.

Dinner

SHRIMP COCKTAIL

BAKED FILLET OF HALIBUT
OR SOLE*

GREEN SALAD

FRUIT COMPOTE

COFFEE

Baked Fillet of Halibut or Sole

- 6 fillets
- ¼ cup butter or margarine
- 1 onion, sliced
- ⅛ teaspoon paprika
- 3 tablespoons lemon juice
- 1 teaspoon Worcestershire sauce

Melt butter in skillet and add onion and sauté. Add paprika, lemon juice, and Worcestershire sauce. Season fillets with salt and pepper and arrange in casserole. Pour melted butter mixture over fish and bake in 275 F. oven for 30 minutes, basting frequently. Serve with parsley and lemon slices. Serves 4 to 6 persons.

A Dutch Kitchen

Dinner

MUSHROOM SOUP

SCALLOPS MEUNIÈRE*

SPICED BEETS*

BAKED POTATOES

CHEESE   COFFEE

Scallops Meunière

>   2 lbs. scallops
>   milk
>   salt and pepper
>   ½ cup butter
>   1 tablespoon chopped chives
>   1 tablespoon chopped parsley
>   lemon slices

Sprinkle salt and pepper over scallops and soak in cold milk a few minutes. Drain and flour. Melt ½ cup butter and sauté scallops until brown. Serve with melted browned butter, chopped chives, parsley, and lemon slices.

Spiced Beets

>   1 bunch of beets
>   1 teaspoon sugar
>   1 tablespoon terragon vinegar
>   1 teaspoon chopped terragon
>   1 teaspoon grated onion
>   2 tablespoons butter
>   salt, pepper

Cook beets until tender. Skin and dice. Serve hot with sauce made of butter, tarragon vinegar, onion, sugar, salt, pepper, and fresh chopped terragon (or substitute dry terragon).

118

Dinner

Shrimps Amadine

    2 lbs. shrimps, cooked and cleaned
    ½ cup blanched sliced almonds
    ½ cup butter
    3 tablespoons lemon juice

Sauté blanched almonds in melted butter, drain, and set in oven. Melt ½ cup butter and add shrimps and sauté until hot. Remove shrimps, add lemon juice to butter, and pour over shrimps. Sprinkle with almonds and serve.

Baked Rice

    2 cups boiled rice
    2 tablespoons butter
    2 cups tomato juice
    salt, pepper, nutmeg

Put boiled rice in pan in which butter is melted. Cook, stirring frequently. When rice is brown, add 2 cups tomato juice and bake in moderate oven (350 F.) until liquid is absorbed. Add more tomato juice if necessary.

Baked Bananas

Peel bananas and arrange in baking pan. Pour on melted butter and lemon juice. Bake in moderate (350 F.) oven 15 minutes. Serve with orange marmalade which has been thinned with Grand Marnier.

119

Dinner

TOMATO JUICE
FILLET OF SOLE WITH
ALMONDS*
PEAS
FRUIT—CHEESE AND CRACKERS
COFFEE

Fillet of Sole with Almonds

  2 lbs. fillet of sole
  juice of 1 lemon
  6 tablespoons butter
  ½ cup light cream
  almond paste
  4 tablespoons sherry
  ½ cup bread crumbs
  nutmeg, salt, pepper

Rub fish with salt, pepper, and lemon juice. Put fish in buttered baking dish and cover with mixture of almond paste, wine, butter, cream, and bread crumbs. Dot with butter and cover with remainder of mixture. Bake in a moderate oven 20 or 30 minutes or until top is browned.

Green and Red Pepper Plate—
Spanish Majolica

Dinner

```
ONION SOUP
SOLE NORMANDE*
BAKED TOMATOES
BAKED APPLES WITH NUTS
AND DATES*
COFFEE
```

Sole Normande

    6 fillets of sole
    ¼ cup water
    juice of 1 lemon
    1 teaspoon chopped parsley
    2 teaspoons chopped chives
    ½ cup heavy cream
    bread crumbs
    salt, pepper

Put sole in pan, add water, lemon juice, and seasonings.
Bring to boil on top of stove, then put in oven and bake
until fish is tender (about 15 minutes). Heat cream and
pour over fish. Sprinkle fish with bread crumbs and put
under broiler to brown crumbs.

Baked Apples with Nuts and Dates

    6 tart apples
    seeded dates
    pecans
    2 cups sugar
    ½ cup hot water

Peel and core apples. Put pecan in each date and place
one stuffed date in each apple. Put in pan and pour sugar
and water over apples. Bake slowly until apples are done.
Remove apples from pan and pour juice over them. Set
in refrigerator to jell. Serve with cream.

Dinner

Broiled Bluefish

    4 lbs. bluefish
    ½ cup melted butter
    2 tablespoons lemon juice
    1 tablespoon chopped parsley
    salt, pepper, paprika

Wash and clean fish. Season with salt and pepper and sprinkle with lemon juice. Place fish on baking sheet and broil at 450 F. for 10 minutes. Baste with butter, turn and broil crisp. Serve with melted butter, lemon juice, and chopped parsley. Sprinkle with paprika. Serves 6.

Peach Cocada

    1 fresh coconut
    ½ doz. fresh peaches
    confectioners' sugar
    almond extract

Grate the coconut. Peel and slice peaches. In a dessert bowl alternate layers of coconut and peaches, and sprinkle each layer with sugar and almond extract. Set in ice box to chill, and serve with lady fingers.

Lemon Dish—
French Porcelain

Index

OF RECIPES AND HERBS

Index

Index